THE
GUARDIAN CLASS

How a Couple Battle Buddies Challenged
Washington's Elite

Dr. Jonathan D. Heavey

ISBN: 0615435416
ISBN-13: 9780615435411
Library of Congress Control Number: 2010918415

He who is to be a noble Guardian of the State will require to unite in himself philosophy and spirit and swiftness and strength...All that belongs to them, should be such as will neither impair their virtue as Guardians, nor tempt them to prey upon the other citizens.

But should they ever acquire moneys of their own, they will become enemies and tyrants instead of allies of the other citizens... Therefore, we must enquire who are the best Guardians of their own conviction. (Plato, The Republic, II-IV, 135)

Dedicated to the brave young men who died before me while guarding their convictions; and to the old men who could never do the same.

TABLE OF CONTENTS

PREFACE

If anyone beyond my own mother is willing to torture themselves by reading this book I would first like to say I am sorry. I have been advised on several occasions by close friends whom I deeply admire not to publish it. Were it not for the dedication I wrote on the first page— and several bottles of whiskey— I would have shut my mouth and given up a long time ago. Unfortunately for all of us, I'm Irish and I like to drink when I write (and bathe, and eat, and wake, and... well, you get the point). Not surprisingly, frontal lobe inhibition and safely filtered commentary are notably lacking in these pages.

What I have written is my best effort to honor the memory of the friends who died before me. I have no doubt that I will live to regret writing about the raw realities in this book, and I have no doubt I will regret exalting powerful leaders with excessive irreverence. The tone of the book may initially be uncomfortable for civilians in academia and public policy institutions. At the same time, for anyone who has seen combat, it will undoubtedly seem far too erudite (I mean complex and shit Manny). Hopefully the sarcastic vignettes and locker room humor will connect these two worlds and take the edge off blood, guts, and explosively disturbing trauma.

The combination makes for a perversely benevolent segue into humanitarian idealism and fraternal camaraderie that inspired this whole story.

I hope this book will, unequivocally, put forth my moral compass and what I value in life. No professional accomplishment, financial reward, or other man-made glory can replace that. When I die, no matter what transient worldly path I follow, at least my children and loved ones will know that I still have my integrity intact. Or, as I would say downrange, at least I'll still have my fucking shit together.

Finally, this story contains accounts I tried to re-create to the best of my abilities. Inevitably my memory is imperfect, and I am sure it will not do justice to the circumstances. I apologize in advance if my recollections are offensive or fail to capture the efforts of friends who were there with me. I did the best I could boys. Here's to you, and to the brothers we will meet again.

The Guardian Class

How a Couple Battle Buddies Challenged Washington's Elite

CHAPTER 1
TURN LEFT AT THE HERD OF SHEEP

I can't say I was ready to see the forebrain gelatin dripping from his skull, but that wasn't really what bothered me. Nor was it his severed thorax, or the strands of heart muscle dangling onto my boots. I had seen plenty of traumatic anatomy before, and declaring the mechanism of death for the soldier we had just dragged from my aid station was no different. So long as the stench of his burned flesh didn't interrupt my afternoon coffee, it would all be part of the routine. What I wasn't ready for, and what I kept picturing in my mind, was when the salad we shared for lunch spilled out of his bowels.

"What a fuckin' circle jerk...look at this motherfucker."

The turret gunner interrupted my introspection and brought my attention back to the task at hand. He offered his color commentary through our headsets as he rotated in a sling above me in the Humvee. As his sweat-soaked ass rotated slowly away from my nose, I could start to see what he was talking about. The lead vehicle in our convoy apparently didn't have the right directions for where we were headed, so a dozen vehicles in our convoy were pulling a U-turn in the slums of Baghdad. Thankfully, when you have Humvees shuttling thousands of pounds of heavy armor and weapons, most everyone yields to you.

I asked where our convoy was headed and was informed we were making a house call to Kadamiyah "hospital." Kadamiyah was a well-known militia headquarters that operated under the guise of medical care so it would be off-limits to our forces. One might think an enemy hospital would be a relatively safe place to go in the combat zone, but we knew that lieutenants in the militant Jaiyesh-Al-Mahdi (JAM) Army had made comfortable homes for themselves in Kadamiyah long ago.

JAM was a particularly ruthless ring of mercenaries who survived by extracting ransom money from kidnappings and killings. In our sector, they had learned to perfect the art of "catch and release" for the prey they hunted. First they would torture their victims, most commonly by drilling holes into their heads or burning their limbs and genitals. After they had extracted all the useful information they could, they would dump the lifeless victim on the "hospital" doorstep. Inevitably the victim's family members would be contacted, and the militants would hide out and wait in lying for their next round of prey to show up. Eventually relatives would learn that phone calls to rush to the hospital for a dying relative were little more than invitations to be kidnapped, tortured, and killed themselves.

I had worked in many trauma centers in inner-city neighborhoods in America, but gang-bang gunfights seemed tame in comparison to the Shia and Sunni bloodshed. As I looked through the Humvee blast windows, I was wishing I were back in the comfortable confines of Chicago's South Side slums, or the projects in Brooklyn. At least there, for the most part, we would probably be OK walking around with M-16s, body armor, and mounted crew-served weapons.

"You've got to be kidding me. Who the fuck are the ass-clowns in vic one?" the turret gunner chimed in again.

Like all of us, he was less than entertained. Some of our vehicles hadn't even completed the first U-turn, and now we were taking another one back in the original direction we had been going in. A dozen vehicles turning like a scene out of a Monty Python skit, we made for one lean, mean, and confused fighting machine. The "ass-clowns" in the lead vehicle were apparently lost. I looked around me at wandering herds of sheep, desolate storefronts, and bombed-out craters from previous roadside bomb explosions. Although the charred remnants in the street added a wonderful post-apocalyptic charm to the neighborhood, I was not particularly thrilled to be lost in this corner of the world. Incomprehensible Arabic graffiti was scribbled on most of the walls, or what qualified as walls for the rows of crumbling structures. Grossly disfigured and maimed squatters crawled on the curbs, warily eyeing our convoy as we rolled past piles of trash, filth, and dead animals. In basic training we had been taught to look for loose wires in piles of trash, but the piles on the training runs had a starting and an end. Here, scanning the countless piles of trash for evidence of loose wires was a hopeless cause—I could only hope they didn't contain another hidden bomb.

"Listen, you fucking window-lickers, get off the short bus and make a decision! Just turn left at the fucking herd of sheep! If it doesn't look right, we'll turn again in half a mile!"

This time it was the company commander. The third U-turn in a row had apparently met his threshold, and he made it clear where he stood on this "Charlie foxtrot" (the military's universal abbreviation for "cluster-fuck"). Even the sheep were starting to stare at us now. The look on their faces translated pretty clearly. You know your convoy logistics are brilliant when inbred sheep look at you like you're the fuckin' stupid ones.

Three U-turns in hostile territory is four too many. As I glanced anxiously at the rooflines, I didn't know whether to laugh at the absurdity of our incompetence or holler at the teenage geniuses who were leading the show. Thankfully no snipers had been functioning in our AO (area of operations) recently, so nobody engaged us from a rooftop. We were fish in a barrel if any JAM snipers had decided to screw us, but thankfully I think we were more valuable as comic relief than as targets. It was nothing more than luck that kept any ambush from unfolding. I made a mental note: *Next time we're going anywhere, I'm bringing my own map.*

"So, Doc, these kids were all fucked up with some shit that made them fuckin' shit all over the place."

The company commander, in a surprising move, had decided it wasn't a complete waste of his time to talk with me. Doctors aren't "real Army," you see. We carry "pussy-ass" weapons like nine-millimeter handguns that usually take about ten to thirty seconds to kill you with a shot in the chest. Real Army men like "fifty-cals" that blow your torso apart instantly in a single shot. Thankfully this company commander was a pretty cool guy. He didn't say it outright, but by his actions I could tell that my trauma training had altered his assessment of me just enough to earn me the notch right above complete and utter disdain. Even if I knew how to crack a man's chest open to massage his heart, at least I didn't pretend that I was anything other than a useless pile of nerd flesh that he had to baby-sit. I think he appreciated my insights into my dead-weight lack of utility, so he had taken a minute to use his most eloquent prose to describe what we were on our way to go see.

"I've never seen anything like it, Doc. They fuckin' shit on the floor and fuckin' shit in puddles of water. Fuckin' shit was everywhere. Smelled like ass baked into concrete in that fuckin' place."

I was struck by the fact that shit smelled like baking ass— quite a coincidence, really—but I didn't think anyone was in the mood for me to point out that correlation. The children he was speaking about had cholera, and he gave a perfect description of what it looks like when it strikes its victims. It is a disease that is transmitted by bacteria living in unclean water. It causes its victims to die of profuse watery diarrhea that has been referred to as "rice water stool." The name is sometimes attributed to the Vietnam conflict where it was endemic. The stool looks less like stool and more like the filthy remnants of a pot of water after cooking dirty rice in it.

Cholera victims usually die of dehydration within days of contracting the disease. Thankfully it is a fairly easy infection to treat with antibiotics, if they are available. Taking a look around me at the sewage gutters running next to the herds of sheep wandering in the road, I was not terribly surprised that drinking water would have cholera in it. I took a sip from my camelback that stored the warm but clean water on my back. *Thank God they can ship water in to me*, I thought to myself. Drinking water that was a hundred and twenty degrees never seemed like such a miraculous luxury before.

En route to the hospital, we had taken a detour to go pick up some VIPs in the Green Zone, where we got to see the biggest DFAC (dining hall) I had ever seen. Since most

Western reporters rarely, if ever, wander outside the "emerald city" (Green Zone), it was little wonder to me that the coverage on television painted a bizarre picture of almost everything in Iraq. To their credit, a news crew had agreed to come along on this convoy to visit the children with cholera at Kadamiyah. I certainly wouldn't want to have their jobs, traveling around the world to report on some of the harshest circumstances that humanity has to offer.

"So, Doc, wait until you see this shit. They're leaving these kids for dead."

The company commander spoke up again, and he went on to explain to me how his unit had stumbled upon the orphanage with the cholera-infected children several weeks ago. Inside the orphanage they had come across dozens of children who were chained inside cages and left to die lying in their own stool. He and his men had gone through many steps to clean the place up and to secure care for the orphans at Kadamiyah hospital. The children had been successfully treated and returned to the newly refurbished orphanage.

Apparently they had done fairly well until recently, when there was another cholera outbreak and the children had been sent back to Kadamiyah. I could tell the company commander was beyond upset with the local Iraqis who were charged with caring for the orphans. I think he would have killed them if he had been authorized to do so. Judging from some of the pictures he showed me, I didn't blame him. He was right. It was horrific to think anyone would tolerate the amount of neglect they had shown to these poor children. Quite frankly, if the company commander had put a bullet into each staff member who let it happen, it would have made the world a better place.

The company commander went on to tell me that the last orphanage director had fled the country after the soldiers found the children left for dead. Apparently the orphanage director had figured out he should skip town rather than face charges or get killed. After all the effort the commander's civil affairs team had gone through to clean the place up, the new director had apparently been no better. He had not been able to maintain any sense of hygiene at the facility, and he, too, was being viewed with suspicion now. Some discussions had been held with local health ministers, but most of the health ministry officials were also leaders of JAM. In fact, Moqtada Al-Sadr had gone so far as to secure pardons for the prior health ministers who were on trial for corruption. He personally bribed and threatened the judges involved to ensure the ministers were let go. All of this made for a delicate situation that required some significant diplomacy to disentangle without causing anger to flare in the local community.

If there was anything I was sure our platoon did not care for, it was diplomacy. Or "fucking diplomacy," as it is properly referred to in the infantry.

"OK, this is the place," said the commander. "Talon-Two, have your men dismount and cover our six. We'll go in to look around. Keep your coms up, weapons red." The company commander was instructing his senior sergeant to take his squad to cover our rear flank, or our "six" for short. He also wanted us to check to be sure our radio frequencies were in sync, and that we had rounds already chambered in our weapons. I was thankful he had his shit together. Any one of these seemingly inane details can mean the difference between life and death in a fire fight.

As we got out of our vehicles outside the hospital, we were greeted with suspicious glances all around us. Our situation was terrifying and unnerving—even though I was the guy in body armor carrying a weapon surrounded by men carrying even bigger weapons. We moved in a loose assault formation, with men covering each flank as we entered the buildings. I couldn't help but think about how this would play out at any of the hospitals where I had worked in America. It certainly would create a huge disruption if a platoon of foreign infantrymen appeared and decided they were going to storm the castle. So far, the JAM guards stood by and watched us, listening patiently to excited chatter that was spitting out over their radios in Arabic. I had been studying the language for months now, but I couldn't understand a single word. I didn't need to understand anything, though, as the intonation of the voices was unmistakable. The guards were yelling at each other with pressured speech. They were notifying senior levels in their command that we were in their territory. The cat was out of the bag.

Our unit climbed eight flights of stairs to get to the children's ward. We all wore fifty pounds of body armor, and carried aid bags, weapons, and other equipment in the scorching summer heat. Each floor had its own shady-looking JAM guards on it, and each time they let us pass, they glanced at us with a knowing look—one that anyone who has ever been to combat understands. It is not a glare, but it is unmistakable nonetheless. None of us needed to know how to speak each other's language. Our eyes spoke the same universal language. And like two herds of rival animals circling past one another, we left a silent distance between our groups, each herd sniffing the other out with the same thought in mind:

Go ahead motherfuckers.

Try me.

As we passed the guards, no man was left without another "checking his six" and his flank. The guards patiently waited their turn while the radio chatter continued on. Not yet, they knew. Not at this moment when we were the more numerous and better-armed animals, even if we were wandering into their turf. They waited for their turn patiently, standing down from the alpha dogs until they could outnumber and outflank us. Then, surely, they would be quite happy to introduce us to Allah's vengeance.

"Doc, why don't you take a step away from those oxygen tanks?"

It was my medic, Sergeant Wakeman, who had been through two prior combat tours. His intuition was sharper than mine, and he spotted things faster than I did. He was spot on as usual— one well-placed sniper round through the nearby windows, and the stack of oxygen tanks in the corner would turn into a very bad day for us all. We were finally on the right floor, and the company commander was asking for the doctor on duty.

In an attempt to hide his identity, our interpreter spoke with the doctor through a ski mask covering his face. As I stood there sweating profusely, I was thankful for one thing: at least I didn't have to wear a ski mask and hope that my neighbors didn't recognize my voice. As if our terp didn't have enough reason to sweat already, he had to worry about being killed later if anyone he knew recognized him. Any terp that was discovered to be cooperating with Americans was, quite simply, completely fucked. He would actually be lucky if his neighbors did nothing more than kill him. More commonly, the terp's family members would be kidnapped, and the terp would be extorted for money. Shortly thereafter his family's tortured and mutilated corpses would begin to surface, and one way or another, the terp would eventually be tortured and killed as well.

"So, Doc, they don't even know how many of these kids they fucking saw—first it was fifteen, then it was eight. The story changes every time. It's just classic *haji* bullshit. Fuckin' *en shallah.*" The commander was less than pleased with the reports he was receiving from the Iraqis, or "hajis," as they are called by nearly every soldier (the *haj* moniker is a derogatory reference to the traditional Islamic pilgrimage to Mecca). He was trying to ascertain how many children had been transported to the hospital from the orphanage. But, as usual, nobody seemed to know. "En shallah," as they say—meaning, "as God wills." Or, depending on the way you translate it, "Who gives a shit?"

I hadn't been privy to the conversation that the commander had held with the doctor on duty, but I did notice that we had pulled the Iraqi doctor out of his call room. If there is one thing I hate to do when I'm on call, it is to come out of my call room for anything. Unless, say, my ward had just been invaded by a foreign infantry platoon. Then I would undoubtedly come out and offer my enemies a nice cold glass of water, preferably laden with cholera.

On-call doctors are usually overworked and exhausted, and this guy was no different. He was clearly upset, and well he should be. Not only did we disturb his call shift, we had just raided a pediatric wing of his hospital and terrified countless families in the process. Any pediatrician I know in America would quite likely burst an aneurysm if anything even remotely similar happened on their ward. Hell, if I use a coffee machine on a pediatric floor without asking permission, they throw a hissy fit. Yet here we were with a platoon full of men in body armor carrying M-16s, storming a pediatrician's ward. Talk about "fucking diplomacy"—you can't invent a better way to screw over any hope of resolving a diplomatic problem.

While the company commander continued to get agitated with the Iraqi doctor, I went into the children's rooms and looked at the treatment they were getting. I was expecting to see a mess and "hajified" crap as usual. Instead I found erythromycin and trimethoprim bottles sitting at their bedsides, indicating they were receiving the correct gram-negative antibiotic treatment. They were also receiving appropriate crystalloid IV hydration, and the nursing staff was taking proper hygiene measures to help deal with the profuse amounts of diarrhea. The nurses also had cushioning available for several of the bedridden and disabled children to help prevent their decubitus ulcers from becoming secondarily infected. In short, they had everything covered. They appeared to be working as efficiently as any pediatric wing in an American hospital.

I sat down next to one boy who appeared to be about four years old. He was crippled and had some form of mental development delay. Despite his physical emaciation, he was simply adorable—his spirit lifted the room every time he shared his impossibly wide smile. I said the only phrases I knew how to say in Arabic: *"Salaim-Alaikum, sidi. Mesa-al-rhear, sholnik?"* (Peace be with you, sir. Good evening, how are you?) He smiled even more, which didn't seem physically possible. The nurse explained to me through broken words that the boy "always dreams he become soldier." Halfway across the world from my own wife and children, I wanted to pick him up and bring him home with me. He was why I had joined the Army. This little boy who had difficulty speaking clearly had just articulated exactly what I had always thought about America. He knew what we stood for and why we were there. He knew we would help him and protect him because we were *American* soldiers.

The visions of roadside bombs and the brutality of combat mercifully disappeared as I sat on the little boy's bed. I took some candy out of my pocket and asked the nurse if it would be OK if he had it. She said his symptoms were resolving, so he could have some candy. He was thrilled to have the candy and showed me a picture he had drawn with some crayons. He gestured to give the drawing to me. The nurse confirmed, "He wants this drawing to you." I put the drawing and my hand over my heart, to thank him for his generosity. He was quite proud of what he had drawn, as anyone with a toddler knows is part of the charm of receiving such a gift. Realizing that I had a dollar in my pocket, I took it out and handed it to him as payment for the drawing. His eyes grew wide as he looked at the nurse and squealed. He excitedly shook the dollar in the air to show to his other roommates. His reaction didn't need any translation. It was precious beyond words. I sat there choking on the lump in my throat, trying not to question why God would put such a gentle and vulnerable soul in such an awful situation. I thanked the nurse for allowing me to visit and asked her to translate some things for me. She was very kind and nodded in understanding. I told the little boy that we would do everything we possibly could to help him. I told him that I hoped that someday I could come back again and shake his hand when he was a big, strong man. He smiled when the nurse told him this, and he made the universal sign for a muscle as he flexed his upper arm. I told him he was the best, and that I hoped that he would feel better soon. He and the nurse smiled in return, and I stood up to return to the platoon.

I looked back down the hall to where a crowd of soldiers and medical personnel were gathering to try to calm an agitated child. The news crew, in a benign but poorly thought out move, had placed a camera with a large light on it into one of the cribs where an ill child had been sleeping. The child rather predictably awoke and started screaming bloody murder. Apparently content with the footage they had obtained, the two cameramen nodded to each other as if to say, "Got the money shot—screaming, neglected child on reel one."

The cameramen then turned to me to ask me to examine a child and check the Iraqi doctor's diagnosis. I had not been authorized to speak to the media, so I declined. I told them that a stethoscope doesn't diagnose cholera anyway—a lab test does, and it had already been ordered. They still wanted me to examine a child with my stethoscope, but again I declined. Contrary to popular mythology, a stethoscope is actually an archaic tool that does little to contribute to an abdominal exam. Yet somehow it remains highly symbolic of medical care, much like the microbial-laden white coats that doctors wear every day.

As much as it would help with the television production value to have an American doctor using his magical stethoscope on an Iraqi child's abdomen, I thought it would be disingenuous to pose in front of a camera. I was trying not to interfere with the on-call physician's ward, and I was trying to understand what we had accomplished by coming out to the hospital. It seemed to me that most of what we had managed to do was irritate and disturb people who were taking care of very sick children.

The company commander did not get the answers he was hoping to receive, so he rallied us together to start to move back out. He was frustrated by the doctor's apparent inconsistency on the number of children involved. I can't say I blame him, as a full head count is an absolute necessity for accountability in your area of operations. In the military, not knowing exactly how many people are involved in a movement is nearly tantamount to treason. Nobody anywhere ever wants to be the commander who left Private Snuffy behind after Snuffy decided to sneak away from formation for some quality time in the porta potty. As inane as that sounds, it is not unheard of in combat. It is like a teacher on a field trip, only on these field trips people die or get kidnapped when they stray from the pack.

I understand how the commander's greatest interest was in checking a head count to understand the movement of these children from the orphanage to the hospital. However, what he failed to realize was that he was speaking to an inpatient doctor and asking him how many children were brought to the hospital. The inpatient doctor will only know how many are on his ward. Hundreds could have come to the emergency room and been sent back to the orphanage if they didn't require inpatient IV hydration. I suspect this information was lost in translation, and led to his frustration with the situation.

As much as I loved hanging out with the JAM guards staring us down, I was quite content to leave their turf before their reinforcements arrived. We climbed back into the convoy as the sound of nighttime prayers droned out from the mosque across the street. The mosque in Kadamiyah was one of the largest Shia shrines in the country, and I was hoping nobody would turn the crowd of incoming worshipers against us that night. We drove down the road as hundreds of people shuffled past us into the mosque. The women, dressed in full body black robes, nervously glanced away from us. The men in the crowd looked suspiciously in our direction. Thankfully, this time we didn't pull any U-turns as we left the slums behind.

I would come to learn two years later that a suicide bomber outside the hospital and mosque killed hundreds of worshippers on their way into services. While I can't say I am surprised to hear that, it remains a disturbing thought to know exactly where it happened. When everyone is wearing loose clothes in large crowds, it is just a matter of time and the bad luck lottery before something like that happens. Thankfully on this night, nobody bothered our convoy while we filed quietly away.

During the convoy's return to our base, I mulled over the events of the evening and how the cholera situation should be handled moving forward. I thought we had compromised much of our own intentions through the way we handled the visit that evening. It was pretty clear to me that the local physicians were providing the appropriate care for these children and did not want us involved. I knew the company commander and the civil affairs team were great men who were also invested in the well-being of these children. They had just put their lives on the line to prove that was the case. They had gone to extraordinary lengths to fix up the hole in the ground where the children were kept in cages. Despite countless other demands and dangers, the team had managed to find clean clothes, food, water, and new beds to help care for the children. I was angry, too. I didn't understand how the cholera had come back, nor did I understand who was in charge of the situation on the Iraqi side of the equation.

I asked the company commander about the water source into the orphanage, and he indicated that he and the civil affairs team had tested the water again and found that it was clean. Cholera isn't usually transmitted person to person, although it can be if people maintain extremely poor hygiene. The most common route of transmission is source to person, meaning directly from the water to the infected individual. That simple fact would become the focal point of a complex international "blame game" that would cause conflict between senior level officers from the Iraqi and American governments, and have terrible consequences for these children.

Since I was new to the situation with the orphanage and it had been ongoing for a few months, I thought I should turn to some local health experts for their insights on it. I decided to ask one of the Iraqi doctors who worked on our base for his recommendations on the situation. We had a local physician who worked in our clinic as a translator, and he was quite knowledgeable about the community. Doc K, as he was known, was a Sunni who was married to a Shia who had managed to survive for years in a mixed neighborhood. He had also gone through medical-school training of some kind before the war broke out. He was normally a very levelheaded and fair guy, but I could tell that when I asked him about the orphanage I had wandered into contentious territory.

"It's a dog and pony show, Doc," he said. At first I didn't know what he meant. He went on to explain, through broken English, why I should think twice about what was happening with the orphanage. "Who do you think bombed the water treatment plant?" While he normally was very careful to avoid any semblance of criticism towards the US, his anger in this case was palpable. I can't say I blamed him. I asked about the civil affairs contracts that were handed out to help repair the water treatment plant. "Who did they give the money to?" I didn't have an answer, though in his usual way Doc K was leading me to answers just by asking questions that I would have to answer myself.

I could see where Doc K was going with this, and I could see where our civil affairs guys were coming from as well. The two were headed on a perfect collision course with one another. The local Iraqi medical community blamed our military for bombing the water treatment plants and then giving out money indiscriminately to shady criminals who didn't fix the water. Our guys blamed the Iraqis for grossly neglecting the children, embezzling money, and failing to keep the improvements we made functional. The televised coverage of children left for dead created a huge international spotlight that made the divide between the two all the more contentious. To the television crew's credit, their dedication was the only thing that prevented the issue from being swept under the carpet like so many other problems we saw.

Taken altogether, the Iraqi anger, the American anger, and the influence of television made for a situation that one day would become explosive. The irony was that each group involved had a legitimate perspective that could be resolved fairly easily. Too many innocent lives were on the line to let bureaucracy and adult misunderstandings get in the way. Our unit had come too far to be deterred by such inconsequential hurdles. We were committed to working on "fucking diplomacy" until we got it right; what I didn't know was just how long and challenging that mission would be.

CHAPTER 2
KNIVES AND GUNS IN THE BUCKET

"Dr. Heavey, would your wife like us to arrange a tour with a realtor so she can get a feel for the neighborhoods in the area? Our firm can ask local experts to assist you in the moving transition so your children will be in the best school systems possible. We routinely offer flexibility on the sign-on bonus so you can be assured your needs will be met for your family at your new job."

I have to admit, the steak was pretty good. Long before I ever had the pleasure of trolling for roadside bombs in Iraq, I was practicing emergency medicine at the University of Virginia and contemplating offers from various private practice groups. My newly pregnant wife had stuck with me through four years of medical school, and three years of somehow even more tiring residency training. I called them "dog years" because it felt like I had aged seven years during each one. Seven years of sleepless nights and call shifts that lasted thirty-six hours at a time had taken their toll. I would have quit and dropped out long ago if it weren't for my wife's never-ending support through it all.

We had finally arrived at the finish line, and as we sat and enjoyed our crème brûlée, I saw a smile on my wife's face that brought incredible happiness to my heart. It was a smile we both knew came from the security we would share together as we welcomed our first child into this world. We would have a nice nursery. We would have a nice home. We would have family and stability and everything that you want as you dream of preparing a place for your child in this world. The new contract offer would be a life-changing improvement, and we were excited to build the foundation for our new family.

"We offer the highest compensation of any practice in the region, and we can offer additional performance incentives. Full equity partnership occurs at two years, which often leads to considerably greater income. If you're up for it, we can play a couple rounds at the country club and show you around town a bit. Would you mind if we ask what other opportunities you are considering?"

"I might join the Army."

Silence.

Crickets.

Awkward glances.

It was the winter of 2005, and it seemed that every day brought another headline about chaos in Iraq. The scandal at Abu Ghraib had just unfolded, and every day young men and women were being killed by roadside bombs. Alongside countless other Americans, I looked in disbelief at the images that came out of Abu Ghraib, and I was filled with rage. Rage that my country was doing such inhumane and awful things. Rage that the country I had grown up believing in was being destroyed so recklessly by self-serving interests that cared nothing about the ideals we were supposed to represent.

I looked around me at an entire country full of people who were upset about these things, and yet nobody could do anything substantial to stop the awfulness of it all.

I knew I had no power to do anything to stop the awful mess, either, but I had at least one thing I could do. I could run trauma resuscitations. I knew what was involved in complex medical interventions—rapid sequence intubation, thoracostomies, and all the overly melodramatic things they love to depict on television. I knew the endless "dog years" of training could be put to use by treating soldiers on the battlefield, and I was committed to doing something—ANYTHING—besides sitting on my ass and complaining about the war.

As plush as the steakhouse dinner was, I already knew in my heart that I would be leaving the comforts of academic medicine behind to join the Army. As we sat in a rather awkward silence, it became apparent that the steak dinner was done. My wife, rather magnanimously, elected not to divorce me.

* * *

"Aw, sir, you know, we don't really track on that."

A few days later, I was in the car with an Army recruiter, heading to the in-processing station at Ft. Lee. I had just asked him if he had any idea what kind of income level I could expect to earn since nobody had been able to answer that question. His answer was the same as all the others I had heard—he didn't know. Apparently an annual salary estimate is a detail that is outside of the recruitment scope of practice. I was working on the assumption that steak dinners were, too.

As I got out of the car, I shook off the chill of the winter morning and stood nervously in line. It didn't take long to notice that I was the odd man out. I couldn't help but wonder if I was making the biggest mistake of my life, and I tried not to look too concerned as I waited alongside hundreds of pimply-faced teenagers. Bus after bus dropped off more kids, each one doing his best not to look scared.

"MOVE OUT! PUT YOUR KNIVES AND YOUR GUNS IN THE BUCKET!"

It was four thirty in the morning, and it was suddenly crystal clear that I was in the wrong line. I swallowed a gulp, tried not to freak out, and started moving in the procession. I hadn't signed a contract yet, so I just went with the flow and "played gray" to avoid drawing any undue attention to myself.

"PUT YOUR KNIVES AND GUNS IN THE BUCKET!"

Oddly, as I looked at the lineup of young men all around me shuffling through the metal detector, I realized the drill sergeant had a point. It never even dawned on me that people would bring their own weapons to an in-processing station, but as the line passed through the detectors, the drill sergeant stood by and admired the growing pile of weaponry in his bucket.

"YOU! PUT YOUR WEAPON ON SAFE, HAND IT TO ME, AND START DOING PUSH-UPS!"

Now, I will be the first to tell you that our boys in uniform are noble and admirable men. But they don't necessarily start out that way, especially when recruiters can't get anyone to sign up in the middle of a war. Apparently the boy-genius ahead of me in line got through the "up to one felony allowed" loophole, and he thought the metal on his teeth would distract the sensors from the gun in his underwear. Fortunately for his own sake, he didn't express his displeasure that he had to give up his gun. He just started pushing, as they say.

"LOOK AT YOUR COVER SHEET AND D.O.D. PHOTOGRAPH. IT MUST HAVE YOUR NAME, BRANCH OF SERVICE, AGE, AND ETHNICITY."

OK, this ought to be easy. Let's see...

Name: Jonathan Heavey

Age: 19

Branch: Marine Corps

Ethnicity: African-American

There I was, a thirty-two-year-old overweight and painfully pale Caucasian in the photograph. How the file clerk filled in those labels right next to my photograph was a mystery to me. I figured it was close enough, though. No big deal. What could possibly go wrong if they thought I was a nineteen-year-old African-American Marine? Images from the *South Park* movie flashed through my mind. I remembered the scene where they planned to invade Canada, and the whole invasion was named "Operation Can I Please Hide Behind the Black Guy?" I didn't think anyone there would appreciate its eviscerating sarcasm on our societal prejudices, so I didn't complain that they had all my information wrong.

"TAKE OFF YOUR CLOTHES AND STAND IN LINE!"

If I felt like the odd man out before, it became all too painfully obvious for everyone to see. Why was I the only guy in tighty-whiteys? Where was the "wear jazzy underwear" memo?

"YOU WILL PEE IN THIS CUP! IF YOU HAVE DONE WEED, COKE, CRACK, OR ANY OTHER SUBSTANCE YOU FOUND FUN IN THE LAST THREE MONTHS, YOU BETTER GET OUT *NOW!!*"

Before I knew it, a dozen teenagers dropped out of line and ran away…in their jazzy underwear. They were so desperate to find the escape hatch they didn't even stop to put clothes on; they just picked up their pile and ran. See you later, one-felony-only boy. You probably shouldn't ask them for your weapon on the way out.

"PEE IN THE CUP, GRANDPA!"

Jesus! Why did you have to sneak up on me like that? Why do I have to pee in front of everyone here? Can you not see I'm wearing tighty-whiteys? Please give me a little space, and I'm sure Mr. Happy can get to work…

"PEE IN THE CUP, GRANDPA!"

…screaming at my penis does not help! I have a prostate, for Christ's sake!

"PEE IN THE CUP, GRANDPA!"

There must be a God—I have no other way to explain how I urinated. In retrospect, it is obvious why that guy screamed so much. He collects piss from teenagers—*for a living*. Every day. For years. Mr. Army Teenage Piss Collector, that's him. What a great job. It turns out he's not even really a drill sergeant, but none of us could tell the difference that day.

I went on to complete what is called the MEPS screening physical, and it was a far more arduous process than I ever could have imagined. My recruiter had not specifically coached me and told me what everyone knows—you just lie on the intake form and indicate "no" for every answer. Pay no mind to the big capital letters at the top of the form that threaten to imprison you if you don't fully disclose every answer—that's a minor detail.

The pages and pages of intake forms were filled with medical screening questions. Ever had a cough that was treated with antibiotics? Who hasn't? I made the mistake of saying yes and was ordered to return for two additional days at four-thirty in the morning for a formal consultation with a pulmonologist. When I acknowledged that I had a simple procedure done on my knee twelve years earlier, I was ordered to come back again on another day to have an orthopedic surgeon look at my perfectly normal knee. I had to provide documentation that documentation from my knee procedure had been destroyed because it was so old. That's right—documents to prove other documents don't exist. I won't even mention what they do if you admit if you've ever put cream on a hemorrhoid. It's medieval.

All this made for a rather entertaining dynamic. As a physician, I could talk collegially with the other medical professionals who were evaluating me. The consultants who saw me were private physician contractors who billed the government an enormous fee to look at a useless X-ray. It was quite a racket actually, and my first real exposure to the level of bureaucracy involved. They knew they were just there for an easy dollar, but thankfully they also prevented idiots like one-felony-boy from getting in. By the end of it all, I had worn a personal path to the entrance of the MEPS screening station and got to know Mr. Teenage Piss Collector on a first-name basis.

The "ascension" process, as it is known, took about ten months to complete, and this was both at the height of the Iraq war and before I received any form of compensation. At each stage I wondered why they were creating all these hurdles for a trauma-trained physician to volunteer to join the Army. I still don't have a good answer, but at least now I know it wasn't just my own inexperience navigating the process that made it so difficult. It's just the tip of the iceberg for the bureaucratic processes involved in government institutions.

After several months, I was told that my application packet was in front of "the board" for commissioning. Sadly, it was actually lost in the inner circle of Hades, which is apparently located somewhere between St. Louis and Germany. Oddly, none of the file clerks in Hades have ever been able to find a working contract, so at every step of my ascension, I was viewed with skepticism. As if, somehow, I was the one trying to pull a quick one to sneak into the Army. No, no, you're right. You caught me. Everybody I know is leaving academic medicine to join the Army now.

My commission was completed after the normal summertime basic training, so I reported to my first post at Walter Reed Army Medical Center without really knowing how to wear a uniform or which officers to salute. My first months there were spent navigating what soon became a world-famous series of dysfunctional offices full of disinterested and underpaid civilian contractors. Upon arrival I was told I could not have my ID picture taken without a uniform, so I had to find a place to buy a uniform. When I found a place to purchase a uniform, I was told I had to have an ID to buy them. Let me say this again: you need a uniform to get an ID, and an ID to get a uniform. Each office had multiple layers of the same circular rules and processes. The only way I can describe it is as if the craziest DMV office you have ever seen suddenly metastasized, starting taking massive doses of steroids, and got staffed by the lowest paid and least cooperative employees anywhere. It was an internist's dream come true—if you didn't have high blood pressure to start with, you were guaranteed to have it by the end.

For all the frustration and uncertainty involved, learning how to make the levers of the machine work was a training experience that would ultimately serve me well years later. The logistical challenges I ran into were also mitigated by a powerful and profound reality when I started to meet my fellow soldiers at Walter Reed.

I was surprised, actually, the first time I saw a young man walking on amputated legs. I was still a civilian essentially. Obviously I was aware there was a war going on, but for whatever reason I had never envisioned seeing a young man in Adidas sneakers and Nike shorts walking around with two aluminum legs. I had only seen images of the war in newspapers or on television, and somehow the mass media never seemed to show the impact it had in terms of human flesh. Charred-out car bombs and remote explosions can't compare with the sight of an injured person. So the first time I saw someone with amputated limbs in person, it was somehow a strange sight to see. And then it happened again. And again.

And again.

And again.

And again.

It did not take long for me to realize that I had been a naïve fool in my comfortable civilian existence. I didn't know any of the guys walking around me, and it was apparent that they were in a tight fraternity of brothers who knew more about this world than anyone like me could ever really appreciate. And here they were, missing legs and arms, struggling to walk all over the same damn campus that had been frustrating to me. It was a reality check that reminded me just how insulated a life I had been leading, and at the same time it added an incredibly important new aspect to the meaning of my work. Work no longer felt like work—it had a purpose that captured me and motivated me like no other point in my life.

One day when I reported to an orientation appointment in the hospital, I came across a young man I will never forget. Half his face looked like it had been blown off, and he was missing his right arm and leg. His left leg was locked in extension in his wheelchair with an external fixator immobilizing it. External fixators are complex exoskeleton-like devices that look like something out of a horror movie. They are a series of external pins and rods that pierce through the skin to the underlying bone, and they function as a scaffolding matrix across major joints to stabilize the underlying fractures.

I've seen plenty of severe injuries in my work, so even though he had injuries that would be quite disturbing to most non-medical people, that wasn't what struck me about him. What hit me was the family walking next to him, and the tragedy of *their* lives. This soldier looked to be no more than nineteen years old. He had an impossibly young wife trailing behind his mechanized wheelchair, and she was carrying not one but two children. Both he and his wife were covered in tattoos and body piercings that spoke to their hardened young lives. When I saw the two of them, they were understandably frustrated with one another and arguing over some kind of difficulty they were experiencing as they shuttled among the various dysfunctional offices.

With all the blessings and resources in my life, all I could think about when I saw this young man was that he didn't stand a damn chance—and neither did his wife or his children. As he wheeled his wheelchair toward the waiting room for an appointment, the tread became stuck on the small rubber ribbon that crossed the door threshold. The rubber could not have been half an inch high. It was utterly inconsequential and perfectly normal for any other person walking by. Yet for this incredibly brave warrior, it might as well have been Mt. Everest. His wife, with a newborn in her arms and a toddler pulling at her pants, was beyond herself. She couldn't help him, either. She tried to leverage her hundred pounds of body weight against the lock on his wheelchair wheels, but it was obviously futile.

There was something terribly symbolic about that rubber strip and the insurmountable problem it created for this warrior and his young family. He had been on the other side of the globe fighting, screaming, shooting, and overcoming any hurdle that was put in his way. Yet here he was, unable to cross the threshold for a doorway. I can't say what he was feeling inside, but I know what I felt like just witnessing it. The symbolism was not lost on him, or anyone else who saw what happened. We all knew his life would be full of obstacles, and the rubber strip was just one small indication of what lay ahead of him.

Now, years later, I often find myself wondering where that young man is. I wonder where his wife and daughters are. I wonder if he can feed himself, or walk with prosthetics now. I wonder if he hates me, and hates us for what our country has done to him. I wonder about his life as I sit in beautifully sheltered classrooms at Yale business school, evaluating revenue metrics on multinational corporations that have made hundreds of billions of dollars in profits from the war.

That brave warrior will never be involved in executive business decisions or international policy analysis. He doesn't need to sully himself with that kind of bullshit. Yet he will always know exactly what he is missing in his life, no matter how the balance sheet equations are calculated. For all his valor and incredible bravery, he will never profit one penny—he will simply pay an unbearable price.

CHAPTER 3
WRAMC

Early one winter morning as I wandered the Walter Reed campus, I noticed an unusually large number of black chrome SUVs parked in the lots. It was fairly normal to see an occasional caravan carrying congressional delegations and other VIPs around, but on this day it was obvious something more significant was happening. Everywhere I turned there were convoys of black SUVs being shadowed by police escorts, complete with flashing lights and sirens. As if, somehow, you might not realize there were very important people inside the herd of chrome-polished-jet-black Chevy Tahoes.

In the semicircle driveway outside the main hospital, a number of satellite news trucks had parked, and groups of reporters huddled to talk among themselves. I followed the crowd of reporters and people into Joehle Auditorium, a small auditorium that was used for grand round lectures and other faculty gatherings in the hospital. As I shuffled inside the room, I was met by a Secret Service agent standing in the doorway wearing dark sunglasses and a radio transmitter worm in his ear. He seemed rather disinterested in me, so I walked by and casually showed my ID as if I was supposed to be at the event. He didn't tackle me or threaten to kill me, so I figured that pretty much equated to permission to enter. I tried not to be envious of his indoor sunglasses and his earpiece. I thought it would make treating patients so much more fun if I could wear high-speed gear like that in my office.

* * *

"What's that you say, Ms. Jones? You're having difficulty with your bowel movements?"

"Well, you see it started in 1972, when I noticed a burning itch…"

(Pressing my finger to my earpiece while steadily avoiding eye contact behind sunglasses) "I'm sorry to interrupt, ma'am. Please excuse me for just a moment. Stay calm; there is no cause for alarm. Someone will be here to assist you with your itch shortly."

* * *

As I walked past the Secret Service agent into the auditorium, I did everything I could not to look completely awestruck. Everywhere I looked there were generals, admirals, senior executive service (SES) members, and other senior "flag-grade" officers milling around, talking among themselves. Various congressmen approached the pockets of officers and greeted them, most often when the television cameras were pointing in their direction. At the front of the room, the lights focused on an elongated table full of nametags for the congressional officials who would be running an inquiry that day.

I had heard several weeks ago that a junior enlisted soldier had risked his career to talk with Dana Priest and Anne Hull at the *Washington Post*. Apparently he finally snapped and told them about the conditions for wounded warriors at Walter Reed. Ms. Priest and Ms. Hull had then written a series of investigative articles that triggered public outcry about the treatment of our country's heroes. I had not realized that the inquiry would be held on this day, so I was completely fascinated to be able to watch what was unfolding. I felt like I was witnessing a little piece of history.

I took a seat in the middle of an audience row and tried not to look conspicuous. I had never seen anything like this before, and like a driver who can't look away from a car crash, I was trying my best not to stare. The situation reminded me, oddly, of the famous intergalactic bar-scene in *Star Wars*. Only instead of C3-PO being approached by an unintelligible alien, generals were being approached by dozens of unintelligible foreign reporters. The Secret Service spooks stayed at their doorway outposts, like mute Chewbaccas, warily eyeing the room and anyone who entered. Cameras from CNN, MSNBC, Fox News, and dozens of foreign outlets were already set up. The cameramen busily greeted each other or elbowed for a better position, depending upon which end of the political spectrum they represented.

One thing that was apparent to everyone there was that the important participants all knew one another, and they all knew who belonged to what tribe. Collegial greetings were passed around among everyone, with smiles that would make a Jack Nicholson character or a mafia don proud. Everyone knew full well which territorial boundaries were in play and what was expected. "Nice to see you, Mr. General" actually meant, "I'm going to fuck you over, Mr. General"; and Mr. General knew full well to smile broadly in return and say, "Fuck you very much, Mr. Congressman, fuck you very much. Tell your wife and kids I miss them."

The session opened with brief comments from the pair of three-star generals who were the primary focus of the discussion.

The first general spoke for less than a minute and offered some comments of a conciliatory nature about getting to the bottom of the problems. When he concluded his brief remarks, the upstart congressman who chaired the committee looked at him in disbelief and bluntly blurted out, "That's it? That's your prepared statement?"

I almost shit my pants. Quietly, though—if I had learned anything during my first few months in the military, it was to stay very quiet when shitting my pants. That way the stench can be attributed to anyone when it gets out.

"Yes, sir, I apologize."

I bit my tongue and tried desperately not to look shocked. A general who had spent over thirty years serving his country had just shown the deference to use the word *sir* to apologize to a self-interested first-term congressman who was twenty years his junior.

The general continued, "We've been working extremely hard to root out the problems, and I thought it would be advisable to focus my full attention on that mission, sir. I apologize that my statement is not lengthier."

Fuck you very much, Mr. Congressman, fuck you very much. I felt like I was watching a Jedi perform his art. The general took the full blunt of the insult, caught its energy, and reversed it back with more force and a smile to boot. *Here is my "apology," you punk-ass little twerp. How would you like a nice cup of shut the fuck up?* The dynamics between the two panels were completely fascinating to watch.

The day carried on with political theater that was predictable and yet totally entertaining. It was the first time I had ever seen something significant happening "inside the Beltway," and it was highly instructive. Each time a congressman acted out in some way, camera shutters would fly and flashbulbs would start popping all over the place. One congressman used that day's newspaper as a prop to hold up as he made a completely inane point. The newspaper had nothing to do with whatever rambling commentary he subsequently offered, but that was irrelevant. What mattered was that every cameraman started flashing pictures of him holding the paper in the air and waving it next to his head. As if somehow it were a magical wand, complete with mystical power and all. I held my breath and eagerly waited for a unicorn to appear, though I would have settled for a magical rainbow or dark sunglasses and an earpiece to wear in my office.

The congressmen running the inquiry knew full well that the generals were duct-taping together an institution that had been targeted by the base realignment and closure (BRAC) committee to be closed someday. Apparently it didn't occur to anyone in Congress or elsewhere that tens of thousands of combat casualties might require additional resources for help. So while they trimmed the budget and back-filled slots with minimum-wage private contractors, the demands on clinical care skyrocketed. The outcome was surprising only to fools who liked to use newspapers as magic wands. If only unicorns could start IVs. Now *that* would be cool.

As I sat behind the row of television cameras, one of the congressmen asked the general what he felt was the primary problem. The general told him it was very difficult to find people who were willing to work at Walter Reed. At this point in time, I was almost a year into my ascension process and the Army still owed me nearly a hundred thousand dollars in salary and other compensation. They still didn't know where my contract was. I sat there in my seat and tried desperately not to whisper those minor details into his ear. The young men who were injured and sitting all around me helped me keep my minor logistical challenges in perspective, though, as usual. What would be totally unacceptable in the civilian world was nothing but a minor bureaucratic glitch relative to the heroic testaments of sacrifice sitting all around me.

As the day carried on, the audience started to lose interest in the comedic drama while the congressmen continued to vie for the lead protagonist title. I didn't know what kind of dénouement would come after such a production, but I wasn't disappointed. Late in the afternoon, the committee decided to do what all committees do—table the agenda and meet again some other time to tackle the tough issues.

At the end of the theater, the various actors stood around and posed for an extended photo session. Each one wanted to be pictured with pre-positioned soldiers who were there with an assortment of highly visible injuries: disfigured faces, burned-off limbs, and other disturbing pleasantries. At the time I thought to myself that it might be interesting for the soldiers to meet such high-profile leaders. What I didn't appreciate, and wouldn't be able to appreciate for years to come, was what was going unspoken as the congressmen shook hands and smiled for the cameras.

The soldiers were trained professionals and they respectfully stood in line, as they had been instructed by their superiors. Those same superiors, more often than not, had no combat patch on the right shoulder of their uniforms. A combat patch can only be earned after serving thirty days somewhere at least close to a combat zone, if not actually in one. Years later I would come to appreciate just how many senior officers in that room had never once seen combat. Years later I would also come to appreciate just how angry that makes any man who has seen its gruesome brutality—let alone those who have paid for it with their own blood. So while the maimed soldiers stood and shook hands with the congressmen as they smiled for the cameras, I am sure there were words that went unspoken. Fuck you very much, sir, fuck you very much.

* * *

By New Year's Eve 2006, I found myself driving through the lawless tribal territory known as Texarkana. I had finally completed my Walter Reed orientation, and I was driving to the officer basic training course (OBC) at Ft. Sam Houston in San Antonio, Texas. As I passed through the borderless frontier between Texas and Arkansas, I passed a sign for a town named Hope. Looking around at the remote surroundings and sparse evidence of civilization, I was amazed to think that President Clinton had been raised there. If ever there was evidence of the American dream, Texarkana must surely qualify. It stood in stark contrast to the garrison at Walter Reed and the elite corridors of power in Washington. I didn't know it at the time, but I was driving right past the place where my battle buddy, John Knight, was raised. John and I would come to be best friends in Iraq little more than a year later, and he would teach me more than I ever realized about this world.

As I pulled into a hotel for the night, I called my wife to see how she was doing with our three-month-old daughter at home. We were still struggling to pay our new bills while the Army tried to figure out my paycheck. My student loans from medical school had kicked in to repayment, so between that and our household moves, hospital bills, holidays, uniforms, and other expenses, we had burned through tens of thousands of dollars in savings. My trip to OBC was official business that was supposed to be coordinated through Walter Reed, but they couldn't figure out who was supposed to pay for my trip. I knew they would never figure it out in time for my OBC training, so I just got in my car and hit the road to fix the problem myself. As I drove, the non-commissioned officers (NCOs) at Walter Reed called to tell me that the brigade commander wasn't sure how to prevent me from being listed as AWOL (absent without leave). It was oddly comforting in a way—being ordered to drive somewhere on my own dime, while also being told I might be charged as AWOL. It made me feel like I had never left base.

I arrived at Ft. Sam Houston and drove around to the various barracks to find where I was staying. As I checked in, I came across a foreign soldier who had come in from Afghanistan. I have no idea how he managed to navigate halfway around the world and through all the language and cultural barriers to arrive at officer basic. As shocked as I was to see him, I came across several officers from Egypt and Jordan shortly later as they sat in the ID card office. These were just a few more reminders that I was working for an organization that was much broader than I had ever really fully realized. I had never even known that our military regularly trained officers from other countries on our own soil. Yet there they were, learning how to become officers from the world's largest and most efficient military system.

We were soon in the throes of our basic training, although as any NCO will tell you, officer basic training is completely pampered relative to the grueling training that enlisted soldiers go through. Somehow it was my luck that San Antonio experienced a bizarre and long-lasting series of ice storms that winter. Apparently the Gulf Stream dipped directly down from Canada to San Antonio. As a result, we did nearly all of our field exercises in freezing rain or sleet. Having grown up in Buffalo, I was no stranger to the cold, but I never in my life thought that I would have to worry about hypothermia in San Antonio.

Eventually I learned that I could sit on the built-in exothermic packets in our MREs (meals ready to eat) to warm myself up when push-ups no longer did the trick. The exothermic packet was designed to warm up whatever gruel was contained in the MRE, and the chemical reaction in the packet would bring the gruel to a boil almost instantly. But each meal comes with only one heater packet, so you had to decide which was more important—warm food or a warm seat cushion. Personally, I usually opted for a seat cushion. I learned to make good use of the extra spicy hot sauce to help make the cold, gelatinous block of gruel more palatable. My posterior was much happier for it, and the spicy sauce almost convinced my tongue that the frozen block of desiccated preservatives was meant to be eaten.

The field elements of basic training were held out at Ft. Bullis, a remote area of sprawling desert tundra just north of San Antonio. The training compound had a series of enormous tents that, in theory, had a heater blowing into one end. It was usually about fifty guys to a tent, and we were never sure how many rats per tent. Our best estimate was about ten. Guys who brought "pogie bait" snacks with them often found the rats preferred their snacks to our stacks of MREs in the mess hall tent. In fact, I don't think any rat anywhere on Ft. Bliss has ever lowered himself to eating an MRE.

My bunk neighbor was from the bayous of Louisiana, and every day he had one disgusting story after another about things you shouldn't really do to wild animals. I felt like I was listening to Bubba from *Forest Gump* talk about shrimp products every time he started his stories. Only instead of slowly listing the types of shrimp on a menu—jumbo shrimp, shrimp scampi, butterfly shrimp—he would list off things he had shoved up different animal parts—garden hose, small rocks, fishing pole. The amazing part was he had a medical application for nearly every foreign object he had used, and a different animal for each one. He used the garden hose as an improvised naso-gastric tube to decompress a horse's stomach. The small rocks were improvised intrauterine devices to keep the female cows from getting pregnant. And the fishing pole that he shoved into an alligator's mouth? Well, turns out he just did that to "piss it off." Brilliant.

Each morning the field training kicked off at 04:30 in the combative pits, where we learned the basics of hand-to-hand combat. Teams of grown men would pile into a wrestling pit full of frozen rubber chunks that were coated in ice from the frozen dew. Wrestling in ice was an awesome way to start each day. Of course, it led to any number of jokes about cuddling for warmth with our wrestling partners. We were all so cold, our camp policy shifted from "don't ask, don't tell" to "it's OK to cuddle."

One night we were preparing for our nighttime land navigation test when the freezing rain began to open up on us. I tried to keep my map and orientation points dry, but it was impossible. We were all soaked to the bone. The cadre leaders sent us out to find our landmarks, trying hard not to laugh at our sorry asses as we mucked out into the muddy desert and brush. My compass was fogged over, and the glowing azimuth notches didn't work at all. I distinctly remember crawling on my stomach through half-frozen and disgusting mud underneath the dense desert brush. As the sleet and rain fell off the brush and down my neck, I couldn't help but think about the dinner my wife and I had enjoyed at the steakhouse the year before. I was trying to convince myself I had made the right decision to turn down the private practice offer. As the mud oozed through my long underwear, I tried to use the thoughts of crème brûlée to keep me warm inside.

Despite the freezing rain and sleet, I really enjoyed basic training. It was great to meet the other guys in my class and gain an understanding about the military. As the weeks in the field training passed, I found that I really enjoyed my cadre trainers, too. I was always amazed when some idiot in my class wouldn't catch on to the simplest directions they would give us. Surviving basic is very simple—just be "gray." You learn quickly you should never volunteer for anything, never be anywhere except the middle of the pack, and never open your mouth unless you are being asked to say, "Yes, sir." Oh, you can also open your mouth to vomit during PT runs, but shut it quickly after that and get back to the pack before you're noticed.

In its own unique way, basic is completely liberating because you don't have to figure out anything complicated. I loved when some fool would come sprinting out of the porta-jon, pulling his pants up in stride, while everyone else was in formation. Invariably they would try to explain themselves. It was comedy listening to their sniveling as the cadre "smoked" them. Just shut up and start pushing already—it's not complicated! The cadre already knows you can't crap because you're eating frozen MREs!

One of the last stages in the field training involved a chemical-gas testing scenario. As usual, it was the highlight of the cadre's day to put us through the test. They tried to hype it up like it was some terrifying experience. As everyone lined up, it was easy to see it really was frightening for some of our classmates. Group after group would come out the other side of the gas chamber, moaning and often vomiting. Each group in the chamber had one or two people who freaked out or had leaky masks. They came sprinting out of the chamber leaking snot and tears, usually vomiting into the bushes as their bodies revolted against the gas.

When it was my turn, I had a good seal on my mask and felt comfortable with my breathing. What I didn't realize was that the acidic gas reacts with moisture on any membranes *anywhere* on your body. Before I knew it, my armpits felt like they were being stabbed, and my testicles were on FIRE. I wasn't going to be one of the punk-outs, though, no matter how many times we went around the hissing gas pit. After what seemed like an eternity, the cadre asked me to take my mask off and recite my social security number. I did so and was cleared to go out the other side of the chamber—which I did rather expeditiously, lest I risk losing my ability to procreate.

I kept my eyes shut as snot poured out my nose, and my lungs felt like they were on fire. I knew it was our last test in basic, though, so I had a little fun with our cadre as I stumbled along blindly on the other side. "Is that all you got?" I hollered out, inviting the smackdown to celebrate the end of basic. I couldn't see anything, and I heard the voice I knew I would hear as I tried not to puke—

"DROP AND START PUSHING, HEAVEY!"

"SIR, YES, SIR!"

I can't explain it, but I was having the time of my life. I had finished basic, and I was an officer. Fuck the steakhouse—this was where I belonged.

CHAPTER 4
INJUN COUNTRY

IAW AR 35-100 SM is ordered to tasker 4-32 JRTC Ft. Polk 03072006-15082006; Proceed via TDY IAW AR 32-4500. POV not authorized. Gaining unit 1-502D/101ˢᵗ AA DIV to authorize TDY billet IAW OTSG PROFIS tasker SOP.

I read through the orders, knowing full well what the cryptic message meant. Or at least I thought, syntax aside, that I knew what it meant. When I signed up for the Army, I knew that I would be sent to Iraq, and it was little surprise to learn that would happen as soon as I was done with basic training. The orders I received transferred me from Walter Reed to the unit that I would go with—the 1-502D Infantry of the 101ˢᵗ Airborne Division.

At the time, I had no idea just how different an infantry unit is from the rest of the Army. The infantry is full of "eleven bravos," young men who are named after their military occupational specialty (MOS). In Vietnam, 11Bs were nicknamed "one-one bullet stoppers," and for good reason. They function at the tip of the spear of our foreign policy. When there is nasty shit that nobody wants to do, they leave it to the infantry to go in and destroy everything in sight. Once the infantry has turned a region into a charred parking lot, then the rest of the military comes through to see the placid carnage lying all around.

Of course, I was little more than a new civilian in an Army uniform, fresh out of basic training, when I received my orders. I had crawled through frozen mud and function tested my M-16 plenty of times, but I had no idea what I was getting into. Much like a father advising his son that having a child "changes everything," there is no way to describe what is involved in the transformation of an infantry deployment until you have done it.

I left my wife and baby again in July of 2007 to join my new training platoon at the joint readiness training center (JRTC) at Ft. Polk, Louisiana. The 1-502D Infantry, or the "Deuce," as it is known by those who have worked in it, is about as filthy as it comes. As an infantry unit, they had already been downrange for extended tours multiple times, including lengthy stints in the Sunni triangle killing fields—Mahmoudiya, Lutafiya, Yousifiya— genuine, awful "shithole-a-fiyas." I knew nothing about those areas, but I tried to learn as much as I could before I met my future colleagues. From what I could tell, they had spent far too much time in the middle of the suck already.

I bought my plane tickets and landed in the remote Louisiana airport without knowing whom I was supposed to meet or where I was supposed to go. I found the crowds of migrating Army uniforms and maneuvered my way into the middle of the pack, waiting to see how our herd would wander. The next day my physician assistant, John Knight, called me and told me he had found a nice aid station for us to crash at. Through the day, I hitched more rides from the DFAC to the Post Exchange shop until I found the aid station on my second night.

When I first met John Knight, he was standing in frighteningly short "ranger briefs," shaving his already bald head, and eating Ramen noodles as if they were the most remarkably delicious gourmet meal he had ingested in years. He spoke in a thick Southern drawl, fit for a movie character.

"You must be awr sirjun," he said between mouthfuls of Ramen.

I nodded in acknowledgement, trying not to look at the plumes of mosquitoes coming in through the broken windows of our "aid station." An old industrial light dangled from the ceiling on a solitary piece of exposed wire that had been hung to power it. All along the ceiling, fine Louisiana swampland insects were aggregating en masse to make a home for the night.

"Pretty nice spot we got us here, ain't it?" John asked with a straight face.

I couldn't tell if he was being sarcastic, so I just nodded along in agreement again. Pretty nice place indeed. Especially if you like malaria and the plague. Then it's fuckin' perfect.

John showed me to the graveyard of cot parts scattered around the shack out back. He grabbed two rusted-out poles and a cobweb-strewn canvas. He started grunting and flexing, in his ranger briefs still, until suddenly a functional cot was together.

"Here yir go...tol' ya it was nice."

A brown recluse spider scurried off the canvas and under a nearby shelf. I tried not to watch it, but I knew what it was. I did my best to take solace in the fact it wasn't a black widow. Nearby, a guy hopped out of an old field ambulance (FLA), holding a porn magazine in hand and wearing his Army-issued square-frame Coke-bottle glasses.

John ribbed the guy. "How's tha backseat of the FLA, Mansfield? Didya git a good session in with Rosy Palms? Come on, say hello to awr sirjun."

Mansfield, showing virtually no embarrassment to be greeted shortly after jerking off in the back of a field ambulance, greeted me in his unique daffy-duck like lisp: "Niyesh to meetch you, shur. I would shhake your hand but…"

"Nice to meet you, Mansfield," I interrupted, trying to avert further excruciating details on his exploits.

John pulled out a wool blanket from the pile of spider webs and threw it on my cot for the night.

"Tomorrow night we'll git out by tha other fellers and ruff it a lil' more, but fir tawnight we got it good."

Judging from the luxury accommodations for the night, I could hardly wait to see what "roughing it" entailed. I was too big for the cot, so I tried to curl into a fetal position to fit between the metal bars on its edges. Like some kind of contortionist, I fit in with the metal bars contacting my head, knees, toes, and ass. As I pulled the scratchy wool blanket over myself, I eyed the gathering swarm of insects on the ceiling and hoped they would disperse when the light went off. Closing my eyes, I tried not to worry about where our adventure was heading.

The next morning I awoke with various kinds of bites covering every exposed piece of skin on my body. After I scratched my ankles, wrists, and neck raw, we drove out to our training compound. We pulled in through the swamps to a plain series of brown trailers on stacks of concrete blocks. I unloaded my rucksack, and John took me inside to meet the rest of the squad from our medical platoon.

"Hey, fellas, check this shit out…we got us a PROFIS who ain't a fuckin' gyni-vagi pediatrician!"

It was a nice introduction to get to the team I would be working with, though I can't say I had ever thought of myself as a non-gynecological non-pediatrician. The guys seemed genuinely excited to have an emergency medicine doctor come to the unit, which was a huge relief for me. PROFIS is the surgeon general's acronym for "professional filler system," and it is the "shake and bake" way they add a medical doctor to an infantry unit. Apparently the Deuce had previously been stuck with last-minute fill-ins who were pediatricians and low-man-on-a-very-long-totem-pole of candidates whom they had generally despised. I was relieved in a way that the bar had been set rather low. I didn't want to be the "PROFIS prima donna" that they had to baby-sit in Iraq.

I quickly came to learn that the JRTC training is a waste of time from a tactical perspective, but it is also invaluable for "newbies" like me who have never been "in the box." I came to learn just how many things I absolutely take for granted in civilian life—like clean water, indoor plumbing, and electricity. Each day brought another regression back toward the Stone Age until things like an outdoor communal showerhead seemed like an incredible luxury. The guys who had been downrange before tutored me on what to expect, and they also taught me some of the ground rules for infantry life.

Ground Rules for Life in the Infantry:
1. Baby wipes—quality baby wipes—can be used for more things than you ever thought humanly possible. Baby wipe "showers" are normal, as is showering in

any public water source that doesn't obviously contain feces. Showering in warm water, in private, indoors is highly abnormal.

2. The word *fuck* is not only a verb, it is an adjective, noun, gerund, and participle. If you don't know what a gerund or a participle is, you're in the right fucking place.

3. The human testicles have been known to spontaneously rupture if not relieved of their contents on a semi-regular basis. If it has been a week, you are carrying a loaded weapon. Safety dictates that you discharge that weapon in a porta-potty. Given the circumstances, porn will be required. Given the scarcity of porn, all porn is communally owned and shared. Given that it is communally owned and shared, great care must be taken. That is all.

4. Meals Ready to Eat (MREs) will cause you to rupture your colon if not eaten with massive quantities of Texas Pete's hot sauce.

5. Human excrement, like all objects on earth, falls at a rate of 9.8 meters per second squared. If not defecating into a cat hole, this acceleration is immediately reflected back by blue chemical water that is highly erosive to human flesh. Therefore, stand up immediately after pinching a loaf if you have the luxury of a porta-potty to use.

6. Boredom makes you do really, really stupid things. Exhibit A: two grown men sitting on chairs twenty feet apart, lobbing one-liter bags of intravenous fluid at each other's groins like a twisted game of penis horseshoes. The game, aptly named "bust-a-nut," is designed to test a player's fortitude, or stupidity. Winners have the

ability not to flinch as the projectile passes through the peak of its arc. They also have sore nuts. Narcotic analgesic supplies are available after impact.

7. No matter how much you may think you are "roughing it," you can always rough it more. Unless you are out of water and using your final counts of ammunition to kill humans for your food. Then, you are kinda roughing it.

8. There are few essentials to survival that cannot be created by combining a weapon, five-fifty cord, and hundred-mile-an-hour tape.

9. If your non-commissioned officer (NCO) tells you to do it, fucking do it. If an officer tells you to do it, you've already missed the boat in a big way. "Smoking Joes" (punishing soldiers) is an art form for NCOs in the infantry. They will make you hurt if you cross them in any way.

10. Senior enlisted first sergeants and sergeant majors may have to call junior officers "sir," but those "sirs" better not forget for one second who the fuck runs the show.

Our time at JRTC seemed to take eternity to pass, but the doldrums were a good preparation for what life downrange would be like at times. We treated dozens and dozens of 11Bs (infantrymen) for "prickly heat"—a condition that evolves when you sweat continuously in filthy clothing and aren't able to shower. Your skin begins to slough off as your pores are overrun by bacteria and sebaceous excrement. It is extremely painful, and it was endemic to our camp. We slept in field ambulances on patient stretchers, or out on the ground with our friendly neighborhood swamp bugs. We nicknamed the various varmints that occupied our trailer (Tom & Jerry, our rats, were the crowd favorites). Our cockroach family, the Leslies, occasionally preferred the shelter of an 11B's ear canal to sleep in. And as much as all this might prepare someone for the austerity of combat, I was warned on several occasions that nothing could prepare me for my first encounter with an aggressive camel spider.

On my last night of JRTC, I received a message that the student loan repayments the Army was supposed to be paying had not come through and were seven months overdue. While I had been relegated to the Stone Age and away from any phone or Internet access, my account servicer had initiated a time-sensitive credit inquiry that would have a significantly adverse impact on me. I tried calling from our field outpost to straighten out the snafu (situation normal—all fucked up), but I could barely hear them on the crackling phone line. The guys from the platoon were busy hollering with excitement that JRTC was almost over, and I couldn't hear myself think. Before I knew it, I just blurted out at the top of my lungs, "SHUT THE FUCK UP!" The trailer fell silent, and the shocked student loan representative on the other end of the line resolved my problem surprisingly quickly.

As I hung up the phone, John Knight and the guys came over to shake my hand. "Congratulations, Doc," said John, "looks like you know how to speak infantry now." I smiled kind of sheepishly, a bit embarrassed that I had been crass enough to cuss out the crew at the top of my lungs. But as far as they were concerned, I had passed the first step in a long process of learning.

As much as I enjoyed learning about life in the infantry, I had little idea at the time just how much more I would come to appreciate once we were downrange.

* * *

"Gentlemen, roll out black—keep any lighting strictly tactical. PCI your NVGs and be sure your weapon is red. Welcome to Iraq. Welcome to hell."

I thought the convoy commander was just having fun trying to scare us because we were a bunch of FNGs at BIAP (f'ing new guys at Baghdad international airport). Ever since I had decided to join the Army, I figured this moment would arrive, so I was doing my best to try to be underwhelmed by it all. *It's just Baghdad*, I told myself, *who wouldn't want to hang out here? If pampered reporters from around the world can handle this place, how bad can it really be?* I had already heard rumors that they made lobster in the mess halls, so I brought my appetite for buttered dip and coleslaw. *I've already seen this shit on TV*, I thought, *so if Brian Williams can handle this, I sure as hell won't have any problems here.*

Those illusions disappeared rather quickly. Our convoy commander was preparing everyone to drive with no lighting on a nighttime convoy along Airport Road—where the last unit through had just lost two men in a lethal ambush and roadside bomb. We had to test our NVGs (night-vision goggles) and be certain that our weapons had rounds chambered and ready. I turned to my platoon sergeant, Sergeant Logan, a veteran with several combat tours already under his belt, and he summed it up for me. "Get your fucking shit together, Doc, we're heading through Injun country." He and every other veteran knew full well that the bad luck lottery dictated the rules of the game. One second you're rolling in your vehicle, the next second your flesh is obliterated and you cease to exist. Nobody could ever know who the next unlucky winner would be, so you tried your best not to think about it. I decided to try to think about freshly baked lobster instead.

As we waited for our convoy logistics, I shuffled around trying to find a comfortable place to sleep on the hard desert ground. Far from being sand, the surface felt more like a moonscape with endless gray-brown rocks embedded into dust and concrete muck. I threw my bags into a stack on the ground and tried to catch some shut-eye by tucking my chin into my stinking body armor. As I lay down, a burst of automatic machine gun fire erupted out of the darkness nearby. It didn't take long for me to stop trying to convince myself that war was no big deal. It wasn't a game anymore— it was life and death. And death had us in its crosshairs. On the horizon, a huge fire was burning, and plumes of smoke choked the air as the sound of gunfire carried on. I was trying not to freak out, and I couldn't understand why nobody was even flinching around me. The other guys didn't seem to be reacting at all. I felt like one of those clueless psychology study subjects, wondering if I was being pranked to see if I would wet my panties.

One of the combat vets saw the look of concern on my face, and he burst out laughing.

"Relax, Doc, that's our shit. Just a fuckin fifty-range and the KBR dump."

I nodded my head as if I knew exactly what he was talking about. Who doesn't know what a KBR dump and a fifty-range are? If you don't know what a fifty-range is, you tend to have a little adrenaline pump into your heart when you think someone is shooting a gun at you.

We sat around for a few more hours on the BIAP tarmac, watching as Blackhawk helicopters, C-130 jumbo jets, and other tactical aircraft floated in and out of the sky in the dark. They had no lights anywhere on board, and yet they floated in and out of the black nightline continuously. How they avoided colliding with each other was a mystery to me. Eventually word came out that our ground convoy had been changed to a Chinook helicopter. All the vets were pretty excited to hear it—nobody wants to go by ground in a convoy at night on Airport Road. The land mines (IEDs) in the road were the most common way to get killed. We sat around for another couple of hours until all the guys simultaneously got up to get loaded. We had been sitting there for hours, endlessly watching aircraft hover in and out and over us, and everyone except me somehow knew exactly when to get up.

Not to be outdone, I got up and started to get my six bags of medical equipment organized. I turned to the same guy who had told me about the fifty-range and asked him why everyone had suddenly stood up at the same time. He cracked a smile, enjoying my naïveté again.

"It's the first Chinook we've had come in, Doc."

Looking all around me into smoke-filled, black-night sky, I thought he must have a headset or some other way to magically see into the future. The hovering aircraft were still buzzing all around us just like they had for hours, and I was completely confused.

"How do you know there is a Chinook?"

"Listen to the rotor chop, Doc, it's a double rotor."

"Oh, right, thanks. Cool."

As usual, I had no idea what he was talking about. Double rotor chop. Right, so there are two rotors. How does that tell a platoon full of guys to stand up in the dark when there are hundreds of rotors and other aircraft engines buzzing over our heads all night? My question was answered within a minute or so as the distinct sound of two double rotor airbus Chinooks came in directly over our heads. I stared in amazement at the massive machines that were coming down in the shadows about fifty yards away. Like two giant hovering Greyhound buses, they floated down from the black night sky.

"DUCK, DOC!"

I was at least half a football field away from any chopper blades so I had no idea why they yelled at me. I was mesmerized by the enormous beasts coming down. I was too busy being an idiot to anticipate the logical result from two huge Chinooks lowering into position. Before I had a chance to react, a giant plume of moonscape rocks started flying in my direction. Like an FNG, I was the only one standing and staring in their direction, as everyone else had taken a knee and turned their backs. I had been so mesmerized I had violated that most basic tenet of the military: always stay in the middle of the pack!

A beast of a man came out of the chopper and started yelling at the top of his lungs, but nobody could hear him. He then turned to yell more specifically in my direction. He was at least six-foot-six and three hundred pounds, and I couldn't hear a word he was screaming at me. Double rotors, it turns out, are beyond deafening. I could tell, though, that he was really, really angry—not only in general, but apparently with me. I didn't like having the great beast angry with me, so I was desperately trying to figure out how to fall into line somewhere and appease him. As I saw his jaw opening and closing ever more aggressively, I knew I was in for a world of hurt. He looked like a cartoon character in a silent Japanese movie—his mouth opening and closing in an impossibly cavernous way, spewing spit, tobacco, and other pleasantries from his rotten teeth in my direction. All the while the only thing I could hear was the thud-thud-thud-thud of two sets of double rotors pounding the air all around us. Putting my ear directly next to his mouth, I could just make out something.

"FUCKING...THUD-THUD-MOTHER...THUD-THUD-FUCKING...PRO!"

He started gesticulating with his arms, and the other men in formation started running toward the choppers, each carrying his two bags. I had six bags to carry, and one really angry giant of a man looking as if he were going to eat my aorta.

I was fucked.

I started running toward the chopper with the other grunts, grabbing the five bags I could and deciding I might have to sacrifice the last bag. I had the two heaviest bags slung over my front and back, and then carried two in my right hand and one in the other. I had fifty pounds of body armor on under it all, and we were running—a bunch of eighteen-year-olds and me, the fat thirty-two-year-old. I thought I was going to die. As I finally got onto the chopper, I realized I had been forced to leave possibly the one bag you can't function without. The bags all looked basically the same, and I had left my clean uniforms and underwear packed in the bag I left on the tarmac. Oddly, the six-foot-six, three-hundred-pound, irate bellhop coming my way had rescued my underwear. I thought that was really kind and thoughtful of him.

As he made his way onto the chopper, he made a beeline for me. I caught a glimpse of the rank on his chest. He was an NCO E-5, technically subordinate in rank, but my rank was covered by a mountain of gear all around me. I had learned very well by that time to adhere to anything an NCO told me to do, so I braced myself for whatever it was he was angry about.

"WHERE THE FUCK IS YOUR EAR-PRO AND I-PRO, YOU FUCKING IDIOT!! YOU THINK YOU'RE SOMETHING SPECIAL, GIVING ME YOUR FUCKING PRINCESS BAGS TO CARRY?!?"

"No, Sarn't. They're medical, sorry."

"YOU'RE A FUCKIN MEDIC AND YOU AIN'T GOT YOUR FUCKIN I-PRO?? ARE YOU FUCKING RETARDED?"

"Sarn't, I'm really sorry. I'm just a piece of shit PROFIS. I'll try not to fuck this up, but I don't know what I-pro is."

The NCO's face changed instantly. He went from a terrifying brontosaurus to a laid-back guy that you'd want to drink a beer with. He tried his best not to laugh at my dumb ass, as the fact I was a PROFIS (doctor) made it apparent to him he had been chewing out an officer rather than a subordinate line medic.

"Oh, shit, sir. I-pro are eye goggles and ear-pro are your earplugs. I wouldn't give a shit but our own medics are always harping about it. You never know when a blast could ruin your hearing and vision, you know?"

"Oh, right, I got that CIF stuff here somewhere. I'll put it on. Sorry about that, Sarn't."

"No worries, sir. I'm sorry about what I said about your mother back there!"

We both had a good laugh. It would turn out that this giant of a man would be one of our strongest NCOs throughout the deployment, and a good friend. I never did ask him what he said about my mother. Double rotor chop can be really useful that way.

Our chopper lifted off the ground and our turret gunners rotated their crew-served weapons out of the hull. Standing with NVGs and blast helmets on, the gunners aimed in various directions out the open doors and bay of the chopper. As we accelerated, the air blasted through the hull, whipping smoke and heat in a blinding blur all around us. I had landed at BIAP in a C-130 jumbo jet that had done a "combat landing" that felt like a rollercoaster. Now, as I looked at the darkened silhouettes of the gunners outlined against the city that was emerging beneath us, I fully realized that we had arrived. We were flying over Injun country.

CHAPTER 5
WELCOME TO THE DUNGEON

Our Chinook circled over the darkened Baghdad streets, shadowing the second Chinook in a tactical formation with crew-served weapons pointed in all directions. I would learn later that all rotary wing assets fly in double formation to prevent enemy fighters from picking off a single aircraft during a movement. The gunners scanned the horizon with their NVGs and black-tinted helmets with blast shields, like some kind of anonymous storm troopers peering through the night sky. They leaned out of the chopper windows and other openings to ventilate their sweat-soaked body armor in the blasting furnace of desert air. The chopper darted in constant sudden motions, increasing and decreasing altitude and banking to the left and right, distorting our faces with g-forces and wind. The other Chinook performed a similar dance that we could watch in our wake through the open rear bay door. If it weren't for the fact we could be shot down at any second, it was a hell of a lot of fun.

As we cruised over the city, it seemed like everywhere I looked the buildings were either smoldering from fires or had portions that crumbled into the desert filth. The roads were pockmarked with craters, and the air was full of soot and other foul-smelling pleasantries. There were a surprising number of lights on as we flew over certain districts, yet other districts would spontaneously go black as the power shut down across portions of various *muhallohs* (towns). I kept hoping nobody with a rocket propelled grenade (RPG) would test his ability to shoot a chopper out of the dark night sky.

When we landed at Camp Taji, John Knight was already there, greeting me with a smile and a miraculously improvised trailer device to carry my medical equipment bags. It was around four in the morning, yet John had not only gone in before me to prep our aid station, he knew I would be the odd man out trying to carry all my equipment. I can't tell you how happy I was to see John after flying over Injun country. His was a welcome face to see on the other side of the globe.

"Welcome to Taji, Doc, it looks like we've got a pretty good setup here. We'll push forward to Justice in a few weeks but for now enjoy the big FOB."

I nodded in agreement, again pretending to understand what "FOB" meant. Taji is a large forward operating base (FOB) where the US stationed significant amounts of assets. The base was so large it was impossible to get around on foot or bike. We took a shuttle to our aid station and living quarters, which was the first time I started to see just how extensive the contractor work forces are in theater. The shuttle driver was a Kellogg-Brown & Root (KBR) contractor who had been shipped in from the Philippines. He greeted me with a broad smile as he sat there perfectly relaxed in his Hawaiian T-shirt and floral print shorts. A pair of striped tube socks and Reebok sneakers completed his combat uniform. The shuttle was full of other contractors, and they were all wearing the same casual-Friday-type outfits. I stumbled onboard and realized I was the only one sitting there in stinking body armor and uniform, the odd man out at the office party.

We arrived at our "hooch" and aid station, and I started to prepare to rack out for the night. We took shelter in an old building with sandbagged windows and reinforced walls. I found a ubiquitous Army cot and was soon on my way to dreamland when John told me one last thing for the night.

"Oh, Doc, when you hear Howies don't sweat it. They'll lob some one-five-fives every now and again."

With my eyelids half open, I agreed to whatever it was John said about some guy named Howie. Why he wanted to tell me about Howie at this hour of the night was a little bit beyond me, but I was barely conscious so it really didn't matter. I fell asleep in my uniform and boots, thankful to be in my hooch with a roof over my head.

I had no sooner passed out when John's reference to Howie suddenly became quite important. I awoke first to a massive concussive wave that shook my cot and our building, followed instantaneously by an enormously terrifying explosion. It was the loudest thing I had ever heard. The sound broke the windows in our building and sent dirt flying into the air all around us. Worse yet, it wasn't an isolated explosion. Explosion after explosion kept hammering the air around us. The blasts kept getting louder each time, marching closer and closer to us. I was utterly panicked, and like a deer in the headlights, I didn't have any synapses working to tell me where to go or what to do. I thought for certain I was going to die. I didn't have time to scream, "Incoming," or to even stand up to run—I just rolled on the ground into a ball in the corner and prayed that the next blast wouldn't hit me.

The blasts subsided for a moment, just long enough for me to look up and see both John and our medic Sergeant Avery sleeping soundly in their cots. Standing in total disbelief, I looked over at them as they lay there, completely undisturbed by the massive barrage of explosions. I thought for certain we had just taken casualties given the proximity and enormity of the blasts. But there they both were—sound asleep as though they were curled up by a romantic cabin fireplace. I couldn't tell if Sergeant Avery had even stopped snoring, since my ears were still ringing from the blasts. Judging from the way his lips were fluttering in the breeze, I didn't think he had.

As my pulse settled back under two hundred beats a minute and my testicles slowly descended from my throat, it started to dawn on me that I was missing something. I stuck my head outside, and that's when I saw "Howie." Howitzers are massive field artillery units that lob Volkswagen-sized "155" projectiles several miles at a time. There was a row of them that had been rolled in to be stationed right behind our hooch, and each one still had a muzzle smoking. Brilliant. I had shit my pants and had my life flash before my eyes because our field artillery guys had put the Howitzers right by the new unit sleeping quarters. THANKS, ASSHOLES! Not to sound like a homophobe, but at that moment in time I came to appreciate exactly why field artillery guys are better known in the infantry as "f–in' F.A.G.s."

I woke the next morning earlier than I wanted to as the heat of the day started to set in. It turned out we had the luxury of a shower trailer nearby, so I used the water to cool down and clean up for the day. The distinct stench of urine infused everything in the trailer, and it was difficult to tell if it was from the showerheads or the toilets. Either way, it really didn't matter too much. Cool water was cool water, and I was happy to be able to rinse off. I wore my uniform into the shower to clean it as best I could, and left it to dry in the desert air and sun.

We took a few days to get our bearings and to gather equipment for our new aid station. I couldn't believe how massive the FOB was—everywhere we went we had to take a KBR shuttle to get around. It was like being in a city in the middle of the desert with a moonscape full of garbage and junk. As we took the shuttles around, we would cruise past massive graveyards full of tanks and other military equipment. The equipment stood like a ghost town of wars past, testifying to the never-ending conflicts the region has known. One night I snapped a picture of a sunset while we drove past the miles and miles of equipment and junkyard trash. The sunset felt oddly symbolic as it dipped toward the horizon. I couldn't help but picture another race or civilization someday gazing upon the same sunset as they stumbled onto the remnants our species left behind.

We gathered materials on Taji for several days until we got our orders together to ship down to FOB Justice. Justice was an impossibly small forward outpost located in a Shiite town known as Kadamiyah. We were slotted to cover new joint security stations (JSSs) as well, which was apparently the Army's new answer to our strategy. We weren't really sure what a JSS was yet, but it didn't sound too appealing as we sat there on the nice big FOB.

We prepped our convoy and packed in all of our materials as we prepared to roll back outside the wire. Word had it that a brand new second lieutenant would be in charge of coordinating the convoy, and none of us were pleased to hear that. "Butter bars," as they are known in the Army, are the junior-most officers who hold a commission, typically fresh out of a college ROTC weekend program. They usually have the least amount of experience leading men in combat, and they also have the highest mortality profile of any officers in the field. Our convoy was a large supply chain convoy with a known date and schedule for departure. Local national contractors and translators who worked on the FOB would often be caught embezzling convoy schedules out to their cousins who were busy planting roadside bombs. I had not been on a ground convoy yet, but given what I had heard about the risks involved, I was not terribly excited about the experience. As we gathered round, the second lieutenant barked out the accountability lineup.

"Truck one driver is Herazo, gunner Wilson, and I'll be the TC. Truck two driver is Smith, gunner is Bolander, TC is Ussery. Doc Heavey is passenger. Truck three driver is Hernandez, gunner is Milke, TC is Luckett."

He went on to name the full lineup for each of the twelve vehicles. Although nobody would want to admit it, we all had ominous feelings in the pits of our stomachs. We all knew that the bombs buried in the roads were the most lethal killers, and large supply convoys were the top targets. The driver was in the highest-risk position, since the bombers knew the driver's seat would be full in any vehicle and they aimed their shape charges accordingly. There was little glory to be had in trolling for IEDs—just ignominious death. Recently Iran had started arming local insurgents with an even deadlier version of the IED known as the EFP. An EFP, or an explosively formed penetrator, simply melted through our vehicle armor as if it didn't exist. Human flesh stood no chance when an EFP hit a convoy.

"We'll have warlocks on trucks one, three, five, seven, nine, and eleven. They should offer some coverage for the even numbered trucks."

Warlocks are advanced electronic anti-IED jamming devices that significantly reduce the kill rate for trucks that have them. Sometimes in civilian life I used to think I encountered awkward or challenging politics in my office environment. Here, where a warlock anti-IED device could very well mean the difference between life and death, I came to appreciate the countless sacrifices that soldiers make every day without complaining. As much as I wished I had a warlock on my truck, it wasn't my place to ask for special treatment. I could definitely see how PROFIS docs would get a reputation as prima donnas, though, as it was easy for me to think it was pretty stupid to put the guy who knows what to do with blast trauma into the truck that is most likely to get blown up. Sometimes in war it is really simple and inane things that mean the difference between life and death. I could only hope that getting into the backseat of a truck with no warlock wouldn't be a detail that came out after I was blown to pieces.

We went through our usual pre-combat inspections (PCIs) and rolled to the wire boundary at the entry checkpoint.

We left the KBR shuttles and graveyards of tanks behind as we started out on the road, rolling on the main supply road through Injun country. Metallic clicking noises filled the air as we all loaded magazines and chambered rounds. The smell of freshly lubricated and cleaned weapons filled the vehicle, and the massive engines roared as we pushed out of the gate.

We rolled along route "Tampa," as it was known by American forces, and made our way South of Taji. Eventually we came up to the border of the Tigris River, which we crossed by using an engineer bridge. Engineer bridges are tactical elements that are impossibly bare, with single-track metallic lanes stretching from one riverbank to the other. The flimsy stretches of metal look like the terracing your tires go on when you pull into an oil change or car wash, only in this case they stretch for several hundred meters. It is impossible to see the metal from the driver seat so driving out on them is a leap of faith. This particular bridge had been blown up previously, and our soldiers in the convoy at the time had drowned inside their vehicles in the river. I tried not to look at the impossibly narrow tire track our driver had to stay on as we crossed the river, so I turned to look out my side window. As I did, all I could see was the filthy sewage water running far beneath our truck. I did not find that to be particularly comforting. I decided closing my eyes was the best bet instead. I tried not to think about the fact our teenage driver had probably just gotten his license to drive on normal roads in America.

We continued south down route Tampa, passing hut after hut that seemed to be made of trash and congealed walls of dirt. The few cars that were on the route moved as far away as possible from our convoy as we moved along. We passed through various Iraqi police checkpoints, with each one full of sketchy-looking officers wearing haphazardly frayed uniforms. For whatever they lacked in their uniforms, each one carried an AK-47 or similar assault weapon. They eyed us warily as we passed by, and the hatred was amicably returned by our guys in the truck.

Our driver turned to wave to the guards with a big smile on his face. "Hi, you haji motherfuckers! Go fuck yourself! I hate this fucking shithole!"

The veterans in the truck burst out laughing, knowing full well that the police and Iraqi Army guards were all dirty enemies. Nobody trusted any of them past the end of their weapon. After we passed another checkpoint, we could see the gates of Baghdad on the horizon. The battalion commander came on the radio: "Boys, be careful here and slow down. This is our top kill zone, tier one, so go slow. Look for wires emplaced under the overpass roads. That's their latest TTP, so stay sharp."

Our gunner cheerily chimed in on our truck headsets, "Don't worry, fellas, I'll see the wires. Just pull them out of my eyes when my head lands in your lap."

The black humor was oddly comforting as we looked everywhere for any evidence of hidden bombs. We slowed to a crawl, though every inch of my being wanted to get the fuck out of the "tier one" zone as fast as possible. The veterans each had their own nonchalant take on things.

"Shit, that crater ain't bad. Last time they blasted one out of that dump over there that got Smitty."

"Ain't worth sweating none of this. *En shallah*, motherfuckers."

"These checkpoint motherfuckers been paying their boys to put these fuckin' bombs out here for years. Ain't a goddamn thing changed."

I sat silently in the rear, saying nothing but feeling the distinct "pucker factor" that the veterans had told me I would feel. They all warned me I wouldn't be able to unpucker my anus for a week after I first rolled outside the wire. So far, I thought they were way off. I didn't think I would be able to shit for at least a month.

We rolled through the gates of Baghdad and turned onto Cubs North, another Americanized name for our supply route. The stench of the Tigris started to blow more heavily into the truck. The fetid smell of sewage seemed to infiltrate everything. Our blast windows were sealed, making the heat impossibly wicked inside the vehicle. Our sweat-soaked armor and uniforms only added to the pleasant aroma in our chassis. My eyes were misting up as I tried not to puke from the smell.

One of my medics chimed in, "Doc, looks like you're feeling kinda emotional."

"Yeah, just so touched by the smell of haji shitpiles. I can't help it."

"That's the spirit, Doc. Pretty soon we'll have you up on the fifty, puttin' some lead in these motherfuckers."

I smiled, feeling a strange sense of relief from the morbid jokes. As a civilian, the mere thought of shooting someone was utterly revolting to me. Somehow the combination of sweating my balls off, trying not to puke, and worrying about being blown up made the prospect of shooting someone seem oddly cathartic—like a great way to express my distaste for all the shit that surrounded me. As if somehow the poor souls who had to raise their families in this awfulness had anything to do with my decision to get myself into this mess in the first place. I was starting to understand how young men who had been through this countless times already would want nothing more than the chance to kill someone. What I didn't understand, or fully realize, was that I had only begun to scratch the surface of the vicious anger that combat creates.

We turned through a series of city roads, winding our way through a series of blown-out curbside bomb scars. We passed slowly through crowds of people on their way into the Kadamiyah shrine for afternoon services. The shrine was a massive building with towering spires stretching up into the sky. Five times a day, every day of the week, it would host hundreds of Shiites for prayers that were broadcast on loudspeakers throughout the town. We went a few blocks past the shrine and turned into the entry control point for Justice. Everyone breathed a sigh of relief as we removed the rounds from our weapons and dropped the ammunition magazines out. Our vehicles wound their way to a dirt patch and we got out, enjoying the change from unbearably oppressive heat to normal desert afternoon heat. Outside, the shrine's loudspeakers filled the air with wailing chants from the local Imams: "OOOOOOOAAAAAMMMMM, AAHHHHHMMMMM, MMOOOOOOOAAAAHHHWAAAAAHHHN, FOOOOOOLLLLLLLOAAAAMM, MMIIIIIIIIIIIIIIIOOOAAAMMM."

Overhead, a huge blimp-shaped balloon floated in the air. Known as a persistent threat detection system (PTDS), the device was tethered to the ground and floated hundreds of meters over our heads. It had infrared and other camera devices that enabled our operations center to perform surveillance on our surroundings for miles around. I had never heard of such a thing, but from that day forward I would learn to look up and check to see if the "balloon was up" anytime I took a step outside. It served to protect us day and night from mortar attacks, and it helped us catch teams of men who planted bombs in the roads outside our outpost.

We ditched our aid bags in our new aid station and got settled into a tent with the rest of our belongings. Our tent, as it turned out, sat on the other side of a blast wall from the National Iraqi Police Headquarters. Our new home was named Justice because it was where the police had hung Saddam Hussein shortly before our arrival. The building we commandeered for our headquarters was Hussein's former intelligence headquarters, where he routinely tortured and killed his political rivals. We would eventually make our home in the basement of that building, living in the very rooms where he had run his torture sessions. As I walked around the outpost that night, it was a bit surreal to think I was halfway around the world in the exact spot where Saddam Hussein was executed. When I had signed up for the Army, I wanted to get outside the bubble of academia. Sitting in what amounted to Saddam Hussein's dungeon, it was pretty obvious that the sheltered life I had lived had already been changed forever.

CHAPTER 6
DON'T JUST STAND THERE—DO NOTHING

There was no A-bomb at Hiroshima, Chuck Norris punched the ground.

Chuck Norris puts the laughter in manslaughter.

Chuck Norris has a teddy bear named Cuddles. Cuddles has thirteen confirmed kills.

Chuck Norris can divide by zero.

Chuck Norris once punched a horse in the neck, hence giraffes.

As I sat there sweating profusely in the disgusting portable shitter, I couldn't help but be entertained. At least the Chuck Norris jokes scrawled on the wall took the edge off the weight of the body armor. The shitter hadn't been emptied in several weeks, so I hovered my ass over the lid as I stood there squatting and sweating in the baking desert sun. It was wonderful. The Baghdad diet plan was working its magic; not only was I crapping like I had dysentery, I was sweating buckets of water. So far Justice was heavenly, if you didn't mind large black flies buzzing up your anus as you tried not to shit on your legs and body armor.

On the seventh day there was light and God rested, then Chuck Norris said, "Get back to work, bitch."

Chuck Norris doesn't wear a watch, he decides what time it is.

Chuck Norris can touch MC Hammer.

Chuck Norris once took a leak on a truck. We now know this truck as Optimus Prime.

Photos of Chuck Norris make good body armor.

We had settled into a daily routine, running sick call in our aid station and treating the occasional case of heat exhaustion. It was actually pretty boring most of the time. Most of the time, that is, until it was suddenly adrenaline-packed and terrifying. Most days we would feel some uneventful explosions somewhere off in the distance, with a remote rumble that reverberated through the ground. The incoming rocket fire was usually pretty distant, and we hadn't lost anyone to a roadside bomb yet.

I finished up my quality time in the porta-jon and started to walk back toward the aid station. As I did, I suddenly felt the ground shake beneath me. That was followed instantly by a concussive wave in the air that prompted me to look up from the ground. I saw a huge fireball erupting on the horizon, and as it rose, a shockwave of noise finally reached me.

BOOM!!!!

FFFSSSSZZZZZZ!!!

BOOM!!!

FFFSSZZZZZZZZZ!!!

The wicked hiss of rockets was unmistakable, and as I finally heard their evil noise, I looked up over my head to see the trail they had already left behind. At first I was totally confused by the way the explosions had unfolded in reverse—first feeling them, then seeing them, and finally hearing the incoming rockets that had already passed me. My mind didn't make the natural connection between the huge fireball on the horizon and the delayed hissing noise that ripped into the sky over my head. I hadn't even finished checking my body armor for shit stains when everything happened. And after two to three seconds that felt far longer than they should have, I finally realized: *Holy fuck, we're under attack.* We had been hit close enough to our outpost that we must have casualties coming our way.

I sprinted inside the aid station, where people were scrambling to gather equipment for a mass casualty. We had only just begun to set up our more sophisticated medical equipment, and we only had two trauma stretchers that could fully support casualties. My mind was racing in preparation for the chaos that was quickly unfolding. The senior NCOs ran in with reports from the tactical operations center (TOC), where our headquarters were using the PTDS balloon lenses to locate where the rockets had hit.

I grabbed my aid bag with the advanced airway equipment, thinking to myself that a field intubation or cricothyroidotomy was going to be next to impossible with the adrenaline that was pumping through my body. A steady hand is absolutely essential in delicate resuscitation techniques, and I had never had to perform anything anywhere nearly that complicated while fearing for my own life. My hands were shaking out of control, as if I had just been in a cage fight with a rabid animal. I stood there preparing to jump in our field ambulance when I heard voices yelling over the radios.

"TALON FOUR, TALON FOUR, GRID IS O-FOB. I SAY AGAIN, GRID IS O-FOB!!"

"ARE YOU FUCKING SURE, TALON ONE?"

"Roger, Talon Four, it's the IP headquarters."

"Shit, Doc, what the fuck do we do now?"

The rockets had hit on our O-FOB, or the outer ring of our base where the Iraqi police headquarters were located. While physically it was only a hundred yards past the blast wall, it might as well have been in another country. We didn't talk to the Iraqi police, mostly because they were a corrupt body of salaried murderers. What's more, by policy, we didn't share medical resources with them. I was actually relieved about that piece of the equation, as it kept shady criminals on the police force from trying to steal our supplies. In this case, there was nothing we could do but sit and wait to see if they came running to our gates to ask for help. I stuck my head outside long enough to catch a glimpse of the plumes of smoke that were rising from their building.

We would come to learn a few days later that the blast had killed several of their officers instantly, and there was nothing that could have been done for any of them. It was a strange feeling standing back from the carnage and waiting to see what would unfold. It was good preparation for incoming rocket fire, though, as that would become an almost routine part of our existence on base.

In retrospect, the photo I snapped of the police headquarters burning looks odd to me for several reasons, none the least of which is that I was stupid enough to walk outside after ditching my body armor, helmet, ear protection, eye protection, and other gear. Any experienced veteran would pick out another key aspect to the picture—I have nothing on my right shoulder where a combat patch is placed. It actually speaks volumes to veterans, as it is obvious that as an "FNG" with no combat patch, I would think a rocket attack is something interesting or unique.

Over the next few weeks, our Apache assault helicopters were engaged in significant air support measures for operations that were unfolding just south of our sector. Our "night stalker" operations occurred under the cover of darkness, where thermal apertures and night vision capabilities provided our men with overwhelming tactical superiority. I got in the habit of writing letters home during the operations to stay awake at night, as the ever-present eruptions and explosions made sleep nearly impossible. When I did make the mistake of falling asleep, the explosions would startle me awake, and it was always impossible to tell if it was outgoing or incoming fire.

During the operations, the Apaches would hover at some great distance away from where the ground-level engagements were happening. Sitting in my canvas tent under the cover of darkness, I would wait for the ground to shake and then count the delay until the sound of the explosion erupted across our base. It became a habit—like counting the time between lightning strikes and the roll of thunder on warm summer nights. Of course, these lightning strikes would occur at random, and sometimes they would flash and concuss at the same time as the massive explosions hit right outside our base.

I remember writing to my family during one particularly large operation when the ground kept shaking throughout the night. In my tiny tent I couldn't help but feel dwarfed by the awesome power being unleashed, even though I knew it was my own men who were protecting me with the missiles they fired. At the time I remember wondering to myself how Iraqi families must feel, not knowing when or where or how the next strike would happen. What if the fighters we were after wandered into their neighborhood? What if a missile flew off course, or had too large of a blast radius?

I could not fathom exposing anyone in my family to the kind of viciousness that unfolded at night—not my brother, not my father, not any grown civilian male. I could not fathom exposing them to any of it even if they knew for certain that the bombs were outward-bound from our own forces.

Taking it a step further, the thought of exposing a woman or child to any portion of the brutality was beyond inhumane. Yet for women and children on the other side of the equation in the communities in Iraq, they were exposed to everything—including the true terror of being the inadvertent targets. It seemed completely antithetical to every American and Christian value I had ever been raised to believe in. No matter how desperately we tried to target enemy men only, it was simply impossible to insulate Iraqi women and children from the tactical realities of combat. War is hell, and may God help anyone who is unlucky enough to have it happen on their soil.

I was never so naïve as to think that our forces functioned in an ideal bubble, with smart bombs hitting nothing but empty warehouses full of military supplies. But as the weeks passed and the explosions continued, I started to realize just how many ways war infiltrates every element of a society—every ground-shaking concussion, every openly displayed weapon, every bombed-out neighborhood ends up permeating the land until the very fabric of society is torn apart. The search for survival leads cousins to kill cousins for fuel or weapons. Dogs kill other dogs that stray into their territory. It is a vicious jungle that no family should ever witness, let alone experience.

Men have known that wicked reality since the dawn of time, but the US military has always risen above the brutal realities of war to lead with principled decency and strength. Those principles are what inspired countless generations before ours to join the military, and they represent the very core of what makes America the greatest nation on earth. As the weeks of operations turned into months, I began to wonder about those principles, and what impact any of us could have on how our military and nation were being perceived in the world.

I had joined the Army with an ideal in mind, and that ideal was perhaps summed up best in a scene from the movie *Life Is Beautiful*. It is an incredible film, and it demonstrates that no matter how brutal an animal man may be, he holds the power to overcome any obstacle by embracing the best he can find in his fellow man and the world. In the movie a father manages to protect his young son and keep him alive despite living in a concentration camp in World War II. The father secretly shelters the boy and convinces him that the whole thing is a game of make-believe. At the end of the movie, shortly after the boy's father is killed while hiding him from the Nazis, an American platoon enters the concentration camp. One American soldier takes responsibility for protecting the boy and returning him safely to his mother.

Call it naïve, but that simple and idealistic example embodies what American soldiers are supposed to be all about. American soldiers are the good guys. American soldiers don't scare women and children, let alone kill them. American soldiers stand up for the disadvantaged and weak. American soldiers will seek out and destroy anyone who dares to intimidate, oppress, or harm those who are disadvantaged.

Yet, sitting in that tent night after night, I didn't feel any of that. Just the opposite, I felt like we were the ones scaring the weaker people. We were the ones intimidating and terrifying those who could not defend themselves. We were the ones throwing massive missiles around in a barrage of confusing operations that weren't based on any apparent principles.

They say the key to survival in the military is to never volunteer for anything. And while I had learned to stand in the middle of the pack by this time, I wasn't about to stand around and do nothing. I was sick of our country getting a black eye. I wanted to know exactly what it was that we were doing and why. I wanted to live by the principles I had grown up believing in as an American.

CHAPTER 7
TYLENOL DOESN'T STOP BLEEDING

"Doc, S-2 says they got sigint that the orphanage is being targeted."

"Could Big Blue source it at all?"

"Yeah, it triangulates to that new hospital down in Lutifiyah. The terps say the chatter is about a retribution bombing."

Despite ongoing night-stalking operations, John Knight and I had arranged meetings with Iraqi health officials to address problems we had been encountering in our sector. We thought that medical relief would be the easiest way to form cooperative partnerships with local leaders, and it also felt like the right thing to do to reinforce the principles we believed in. Unfortunately, the report out of our S-2 intelligence team that morning was introducing us to the harsh realities of medical relief in a combat zone.

After I had gone out to assess the orphans with cholera at Kadamiyah hospital, our civil affairs team had been working with our Iraqi Army counterparts to address the problems there and in the IDP camps ("IDP" was the government acronym for "internally displaced persons," or war refugees). To date, our efforts had not gone well, to say the least. The news about bomb threats out of the intelligence office that morning was the end result of weeks of wrangling and arguing among the various parties involved. It was not altogether a surprise to hear that our efforts were prompting someone on the other side of the table to plan retribution bombings.

After my outing to the Kadamiyah hospital, we had met with Colonel M[1], the Iraqi Army brigade surgeon, and several members of his staff who had helped in the initial efforts to rebuild the orphanage months earlier. In retrospect, what was a fairly simple question of institutional authority and control was somehow lost in translation, and our attempts to help the situation compounded the already significant problems at hand.

After Colonel M and the civil affairs team had made their first attempts to rebuild the orphanage, a new director was appointed by the Ministry of Health (MOH). Colonel M and his men reported to the ministry of defense, and the two had no institutional overlap. Unfortunately, the Iraqi MOH had already been corrupted from the inside out, with prior MOH directors fleeing the country after embezzling untold sums of money. Years later, in 2010, I would stumble upon a buried news story on MSNBC that spoke volumes about the situation we experienced in our efforts:

MSNBC Article 6 March 2010

In a clear provocation to the Sunnis, former Deputy Health Minister Hakim al-Zamili, one of two

---

[1] Name modified for security

> *former government officials accused of allowing Shiite death squads to use ambulances and government hospitals to carry out kidnappings and killings, is running for parliament in the Shiite-led coalition led by the Supreme Council and the Sadrists. The charges against the two were dropped two years ago.*

I might add the not-insignificant detail that the charges against the two prior MOH directors were dropped only after Moqtada Al-Sadr himself threatened and bribed the judge in the cases. In a classic mafia move, Al-Sadr allegedly put out hit squads with orders to kill the judge, while simultaneously sending out his lieutenants with envelopes full of cash to help make the options in the matter clear. Fat Tony doesn't want to put concrete in your shoes, Mr. Judge, he wants to give your family some money. So take the money, and make sure your shoes don't get too tight. Capiche?

Colonel M and his team had no institutional authority to control the situation at the orphanage, but he was also our only significant contact with the ability to assess it. Our attempts to rectify the situation by giving him control over the orphanage went absolutely nowhere. We tried to facilitate projects for him and arrange mutually beneficial projects, but a combination of "en shallah" attitude and bitter infighting left him worse off after our efforts than when we started.

For example, in an effort to show good faith, we tried for months to get him an X-ray machine. I finally wrote a letter home about the X-ray escapades when it became apparent just how ridiculous that simple objective was to complete:

The Story of an X-ray Machine in Iraq

It seems like simple enough of a concept: find an X-ray machine for an Iraqi Army surgeon to use in his trauma first aid station. Your mission, should you choose to accept it, is to navigate the morass of bureaucracy involved in procuring a simple piece of medical equipment to improve the capacity of the Iraqi Army. This message will self-destruct in thirty seconds.

Colonel M is a rare exception—an Iraqi physician who stayed here and is now serving in the Iraqi Army. He even found an X-ray machine a few years ago on his own, but he couldn't find a team to build lead walls around it so it could be used. To help out, we tried to either find a construction team or buy a new portable machine that is easier to use. The lead aprons that you often see in US hospitals (an easy workaround) were not available anywhere, and they also weren't practical as a long-term solution in the heat of the desert.

So we asked our boss for some help, and he asked his boss, who asked Colonel M's boss about procuring an X-ray machine or some lead walls. It dawned on Colonel M's boss that there must be an old X-ray machine, and he started to wonder what else Colonel M had managed to protect and find for his aid station. That's when Colonel M's boss ordered the functioning lab and dental equipment to be removed from his aid station, to go sit and lie in waste at his boss's headquarters. Boy, we helped that situation.

Colonel M may have started with a lab, dental chair, and a dysfunctional X-ray machine, but by the time we were done "helping," his boss had stolen everything but the unusable X-ray machine.

So we told our boss's boss that Colonel M's boss is abusing equipment. Our boss's boss isn't from our unit in the new "plug and play transformation" of the Army, so he doesn't particularly care what we say. In fact, he is rather annoyed that officers from two rungs below his office have even bothered to call him. But he looks into it and finds out Colonel M's boss's boss wants Colonel M's boss to keep the dental and lab equipment since it makes him look good to his superiors. So there's nothing our boss's boss can do about it without going through the Ministry of Health in the Iraqi cabinet or possibly the Ministry of Defense—though it is entirely unclear who runs what in either cabinet post.

So we start to look into the Ministry of Health connection, and we find out the last director just got released from prison after a stacked judge and jury exonerated him on charges of murder, kidnapping, torture, embezzlement, and extortion. Other than those charges, he is a peach of a guy. Apparently he was a primary coordinator for JAM operations, and came up with the great idea of using the few hospitals that remain as coordination centers for JAM operations. Did you hear about the one where the ambulance was actually a weapons truck and a portable VBIED (bomb) that slaughtered hundreds of innocent people? That's our guy, and now he is innocent, too.

> *Hmm...OK. So, in review, we can't go to*
> *Colonel M's boss, or his boss's boss, to help. We*
> *can't go to the boss of the bosses' boss in either cabinet*
> *post, since even if they knew whom to contact, there*
> *is a very good chance that person is plotting to kill*
> *us and anyone we know. Maybe, assuming the prime*
> *minister isn't trying to kill us, he could authorize the*
> *purchase of an X-ray machine.*
> *And so it goes—welcome to the vortex.*

Incredibly, the orphanage was just the tip of the iceberg. Every day our line medics would be approached by impoverished locals who were desperately seeking help for their children who had complex medical problems that were far beyond the scope of our treatment capacities. We had asked the National Iraqi Assistance Center (NIAC) for help for these children with awful medical problems, but it turned out the NIAC was little more than a cruel joke of an office with a total of three officers working there.

The National Iraqi Assistance Center had only *one* doctor and was little more than a trailer bunkered down in the Green Zone. I couldn't believe it! The only official humanitarian relief organization being jointly run by the Iraqi government, and the American government had ONE, I repeat, ONE person who self-identified as a physician. I say "self-identified" because I don't think she was even a real physician. She just slept at a Holiday Inn and convinced the other two non-medical military officers that she was a physician so she could get an American visa and escape the country. To top off the absurdity of her situation, she was also theoretically responsible for maintaining health standards in all the Iraqi prisons at the time. That job alone would take a small army of physicians to accomplish, yet there she was, as the only person managing the countless cases of children who desperately needed advanced humanitarian relief and medical care.

After realizing that the NIAC only had one medical contact, we started to build our own database of children and their case files to organize the influx of requests we were facing. I made multiple attempts to procure care for the kids at our American combat support hospital, but I was informed that the medical rules of engagement (MEDROE) severely limited our ability to bring local national children to the combat support hospital (CSH). While there are legitimate reasons why the MEDROE exist, it was incredibly frustrating to be told by superiors above our division that policy essentially precluded tertiary care treatment for kids in our sector.

To this day, I doubt most Americans realize that the MEDROE stand in stark contrast to the Hippocratic oath, and often severely restrict the care our military physicians can provide in theater. This was the first time it dawned on me that the political discussion about engaging the hearts and minds of local populations was disconnected from the ground level realities. If we actually care about winning the hearts and minds of local populations, what could possibly be the explanation for restricting our physicians from providing advanced medical care for their children?

Cooperative medical engagements (CMEs) were the only authorized option for humanitarian relief effort. Unfortunately a CME is little more than a bunch of line medics with aid bags handing out Tylenol and Motrin to desperate families. CMEs do more harm than good, yet they were the only authorized means of reaching out to the local community. Tylenol, it turns out, doesn't help children who have been in horrific bombings and trauma. It seems to take something more to help full thickness burns, thoracic escharotomies, and severe extremity contractures. It was hard enough to provide clean water and vaccines in the combat environment. The more barriers we ran into, the more it became obvious that any attempt at advanced surgical care would not be possible in theater without direct authorization from our combat support hospital directors. The CSH directors were compassionate leaders, but they were stretched far beyond their means. Their mission wasn't to reach out to local nationals. It was to save soldiers' lives, which was a massive undertaking in and of itself.

When the S-2 intelligence officer finally told us that the orphanage with the cholera outbreak was being targeted for retribution bombings, it was basically the straw that broke the camel's back. *Fine*, I thought. *Nobody wants to deal with these problems? Fine. John Knight and I will do it ourselves.*

There is an old saying in the Army training that is designed to guide soldiers when they face insurmountable challenges: "Improvise, adapt, and overcome." So that is what John and I decided to do. We took our frustration, let it stew for a bit, and then channeled into it into the most positive outlet we could think up. Sitting in the bombed-out remnants of Saddam Hussein's dungeon, we would talk for hours about what we could possibly do to change anything. And then one day, it dawned on us. From a basement "dungeon" on the other side of the world, our idea was born.

* * *

"Sure, we'd be happy to do anything possible. Just send them over. Our CEO will figure out the funding later."

"Anything you need, just bring them here and we'll figure out the rest."

"Heavey, we would love to help out. If you can get them out, we'll take it from there."

I sat reading the messages from the satellite connection in disbelief. I was overwhelmed to see the incredibly generous responses. The idea that John and I had come up with was not that unique or earth shattering. In fact, it seemed perfectly obvious, if nearly impossible to implement. We had decided that if our combat support hospital couldn't do more to help kids in our sector, and the NIAC clearly couldn't do anything to help kids anywhere, then we might as well try to ask university hospitals back home if they could help out.

The night before, I had sat down and composed dozens of e-mails to old friends in academic medicine to see if any of them might consider performing surgeries. Our satellite connection only worked if the weather cooperated, if the satellite was in the right location in orbit, and if we had power. That trifecta only rarely came together, so I had to have things set up to work at any moment when everything worked correctly. I loaded up the messages in my outbox, and each went slowly out, one by one, throughout the night. I had to be careful not to attach anything—even a signature graphic—or the messages wouldn't make it. The next morning the satellite feed was cycling on- and offline, and each time it did, I saw another message that was full of encouraging news.

I thought I might be able to ask a favor or cash in some chips with a few old friends, but I never expected the outpouring of incredibly generous offers we got in reply. To a person, each surgeon replied with an offer to help alleviate the circumstances

John and I were encountering, and not one of them even asked about funding for the surgeries.

I had contacted old friends from residency, almost all of whom were now full faculty members at different universities. The surgeries I had written to them about—advanced tertiary care interventions with incredibly challenging surgical requirements—could easily cost over fifty thousand dollars apiece. I thought I would be troubling old friends whom I hadn't written to for too long with an impossible request, yet message by message, it was the same. Not only were they willing to consider performing the surgeries, they were excited to do so without a penny of compensation.

It was the first glimmer of good news that John and I had gotten in months. And while we were sitting there surrounded by filth and carnage, it was the glimmer we needed to keep us going. We nicknamed the project "Patients Without Borders," laughing at the grandiose absurdity to think our little initiative could ever amount to anything. I would tell anyone who was unfortunate enough to be stuck listening to my delusions that we were building a charity that would run in parallel to the multimillion-dollar organization Doctors Without Borders. Since nobody could coordinate the means to safely bring in Doctors Without Borders, it seemed perfectly logical to build a program where the patients were transported to doctors instead. The only difference, of course, was that our budget was the size of our coffee change jar in the aid station, and our patients had to dodge bombs and bullets on their way to the doctor's office on the other side of the globe.

Doctors Without Borders, Unicef, the UN, and countless other NGOs (non-governmental organizations) had all been forced to shut down operations in Iraq years before we arrived. After the Red Cross headquarters was bombed, nobody had been able to function safely in theater due to the constant death threats against humanitarian relief organizations. Both John and I loved to joke that anytime we hung out to talk in the dungeon, we were, in effect, holding a board meeting of the largest NGO in theater. That is unless, of course, you count the Iraqi parliament itself as a non-governmental organization. Judging by its dysfunction, we thought they probably had us beat.

Over the next several weeks, I used the satellite connection to send out dozens of e-mails to old friends from Dartmouth who worked as attorneys in New York. One friend in particular, Rachel Gilliar, took considerable time out of her professional duties to help coordinate the legal infrastructure we needed. She helped craft the necessary forms and paperwork to file a formal 501(c)3 nonprofit foundation, and my wife, Melissa, pulled off the rest of the miracles to make it happen. Melissa handled countless phone calls pertaining to the legal documents involved while taking care of our one-year-old daughter by herself. Melissa was a superwoman with never-ending energy and inspiration who spearheaded the incorporation for the foundation. Invariably she would be asked for a signature from me for some document or another, and she would have to convince the recipient that she was my durable power of attorney. I lost track of how many trips she made to the local notary and Kinko's. In the dead of a Michigan winter, she would pack up our daughter and make trips to the county register, the post office, Kinko's, the Commerce Department, the Better Business Bureau, and numerous other locations in order to coordinate the legal documents for the project.

It turns out that forming a domestic 501(c)3 nonprofit, let alone a nonprofit that functions internationally and has active-duty officers sitting on its board, is a massive legal undertaking. Within a few weeks it became apparent that the 501(c)3 would not be formalized for at least a year due to the congressional regulations and other barriers involved. We went ahead with our efforts, and refused to let the legal obstacles detract from our little project. John and I held a board meeting in the dungeon to decide on our official mission statement, and we adopted the "Starfish Story" as the inspiration for our new foundation.

I had heard the "Starfish Story" once from a friend in college who had inspired me to keep working on a project that had seemed completely impossible at the time. The project started when students on our campus were told they couldn't exercise in the varsity gym due to overcrowding with the varsity team practices. A new gym for non-varsity students was projected to cost upwards of a million dollars, which, of course, no student could afford. Our pleas to the college for help with the project had gone unheard, so we came up with a creative workaround to the problem. We decided we would collect pennies from the student body as "loans" to the college deans who were stating that they couldn't afford to build the gym. When the student body caught wind of the project, they started donating pennies in droves. We collected over seventy-two thousand pennies that we stacked in a massive pyramid on the deans' doorstep. A local newspaper took a picture of the "penny pyramid," and a wealthy alumnus saw it. Within a week, the alumnus made a huge donation to build a new gym on campus. It was absolutely amazing. We had gone from having nothing to accomplishing a significant goal that everybody had thought was completely impossible.

When John and I first discussed the Patients Without Borders concept, it occurred to me that we were talking about the exact same parallel. We were trying to tackle a problem that we felt strongly about personally, yet it was way out of our league and nobody at senior levels had any solution either. At the same time, we both knew that the problem could be solved if we just got to work and started building a solution. We didn't have funding, but we believed in the old inspirational adage "if you build it they will come." To start our mission, I got onto the satellite connection and put up a simple Web site with the "Starfish Story" on it:

> *One day a man was walking along the beach when he noticed a boy picking something up and gently throwing it into the ocean. Approaching the boy, he asked, "What are you doing?" The youth replied, "Throwing starfish back into the ocean. The surf is up and the tide is going out. If I don't throw them back, they'll die."*
>
> *"Son," the man said, "don't you realize there are miles and miles of beach and hundreds of starfish? You can't make a difference!" After listening politely, the boy bent down, picked up another starfish, and threw it back into the surf. Then, smiling at the man, he said, "I made a difference for that one."*
> —The Starfish Story (Loren Eisley)

As melodramatic as it may sound, the story embodied what we were trying to do. We were putting together the pieces to figure out a way to get our first starfish back in the ocean. What I didn't know at the time, and what I wouldn't fully appreciate for several more years after that, was just how challenging that process would be.

CHAPTER 8
THE DEATH BIN

As time progressed and the weather changed, our unit began experiencing more and more casualties from combat operations. The roadside bombs and rocket attacks would pick up any time sandstorms forced us to bring down the PTDS surveillance blimp over our base. The weather would also prevent the Predator drones from flying patrols over our sector, so the JAM fighters could operate freely without being seen. During the sandstorm "brownouts," they would launch rockets into the heart of our base. After brownouts, the roads would be full of explosive landmines as well. The combination gave us all the more inspiration to enjoy the lovely weather.

During one week, we lost five men in five days, each to a separate incident that had several other trauma casualties involved. I remember when I was a civilian at home in America, I would see casualty counts, and quite frankly I was usually underwhelmed by their significance. They were just numbers from a faraway land and faraway people. While I felt bad about the deaths, I never knew anyone who was harmed in the war. I underestimated, in a profound way, just how angry I would become by seeing my men die before me.

Around this time I decided I should write journal entries more regularly so I would never forget the feelings I went through whenever soldiers died in my aid station. I started my first after Albert B[2] was killed. Albert B was a promising young medic whom I had met in our pre-deployment training. I had been impressed by his intellect and motivation. I had come to know and love the guys in the unit, but Albert B... Albert B in particular was going somewhere special. When I first met him, we talked for a bit and he eventually asked me about an accelerated surgical training program at Northwestern University. It is a great program that cuts considerable time out of the traditional physician training path. Very few people are aware the elite program exists, and most students who do know about it come from medical families where the parents themselves are physicians. Yet, as a fresh-faced teenager, Albert B had asked me about it to see if I knew how the Army could sponsor his participation in the program. He was hardworking and bright, and everyone around him could sense he was on a trajectory upward. He was committed to improving himself through his education.

And then one day he was killed. No warning. No chance for resuscitation. No glory of battle. No nothing. Just awful blood and carnage. In one heartbeat, he is a dynamic, bright young kid; the next heartbeat, he is dead. He was killed instantly by a bomb that came out of nowhere and destroyed his vehicle. We heard little more than a dull, distant thud, and with that, his life was suddenly and tragically over.

We hold memorial services for all soldiers who are killed, and during Albert B's memorial I sat and watched the hundreds

---

[2] Unfortunately, I was not able to contact family members for this brave young soldier or his fellow soldiers who were killed. In an effort to respect their privacy and honor their sacrifice, the soldiers' names are modified.

of young soldiers filing in to pay tribute to him. I wrote in my journal later that night:

where are the men among these boys?

one by one they filed out. many not old enough to shave. all of them old enough to know the way their world now works. it works with three less men among them. three less men who were forced to grow up too fast, and die too soon. they are all men, of course. all thrown into an abysmal cluster fuck of humanity by old men who care not.

so as these boys die before me, i would ask you, America, where the hell are the men? where are the men who have turned these boys into soldiers who know most of the burdens of the world and little of the joy of life? wise beyond their years, may they never grow old like you to repeat the same mistakes. may they grow to be insightful. may they grow to understand the complexity of this world and somehow find beauty in it once again.

you cannot rob them of that. no matter how hard you may try. you have robbed three families of husbands, brothers, sons. but you cannot rob these men from becoming boys again. and believing in a world where the misery you have unleashed upon them holds no power over their indomitable souls.

i'm sorry, Prad. i'm sorry, Albert B, Micheal M, and Bryan B, i'm sorry.

After Albert B's memorial service I sat and stared, just soaking up the tragedy of the day's event. I couldn't sleep, even though I knew I needed to try to settle down for some rest. It seemed like my head had just hit the pillow when, out of nowhere:

BOOOM!!!
BOOOM!!!
BOOOM!!!

The windows shattered and my door slammed open as the concussive wave popped my ears. Half-naked, I jumped out of my cot, realizing that we would have casualties rolling in any second to the trauma station. The chaos was instantaneous

"GET THE FUCKING GRID! GET THE FUCKING GRID!"

"SARN'T MAJOR...WHERE IS SARN'T MAJOR?"

"IT'S ON FIRE. WE NEED FIRE AND CASEVAC NOW!!"

"CASEVAC TO WHAT CCP?"

"DOC, WHO THE FUCK IS ON CASEVAC? WE NEED STRETCHERS!"

"TOWER ONE, THIS IS BASE. WE HAVE FIRE AND NEED EYES ON TARGET."

"BASE, THIS IS TOWER ONE, FIRE IS BY IFOB TENT—IFOB TENT IS SHREDDED."

"CASUALTIES ARE RUNNING FROM TENT...THEY NEED CASEVAC STAT!"

"FUCK THE CCP...CASEVAC THEM STRAIGHT IN. GET THEM IN HERE NOW!"

My mind was racing as I tried to think of what we needed to do for the oncoming wave of casualties. We had three trauma stretchers. Turn on the suction, turn on the oxygen, draw up the etomidate and succinylcholine paralytic, function check the direct laryngoscope, break open the cricothyroidotomy tray, spike the crystalloid IV, lace the endotracheal tube stylet, prep the thoracotomy procedure tray...

"WHERE THE FUCK ARE THE RIB SPREADERS?"

As I moved, I realized my hands were shaking violently. I wasn't panicked, but I physically could not hold my hands still. The endotracheal tube fell out of its packaging onto the dirty floor. I quickly grabbed another. I took repeated deep breaths as I aimed my syringes to draw up the medicines, concentrating all my energy to hit the soft plastic top where the needles went into the medicine bottles and not my own fingers.

"DOC, I DON'T KNOW HOW MANY BUT IT HIT THE FUCKING SLEEPING TENT!"

I knew this was going to be bad. The tent usually had a dozen men in it at any given time. I had been lucky enough to be moved out of it just a few weeks earlier.

One of my line medics came running, and as he emerged, we could see he had a body draped over his shoulders in a fireman's carry. He had run a hundred yards or more through thick gravel with a man draped over his shoulders like a lifeless doll. He dumped the first casualty into our triage bay.

"THIS GUY IS OK, HE JUST NEEDS HELP!"

And with that the medic was gone, running back to the flaming chaos. I looked at the stunned patient and, mercifully, the medic was right. His airway was intact. He had shrapnel wounds that were bleeding, but they clearly weren't from an arterial source. His uniform was shredded and charred. He was in shock, but not from hemorrhagic hypovolemia that comes from massive blood loss. A group of medics got him onto the stretcher and he looked up to the ceiling. I stood over his head, and his eyes turned up to me. Over years of training you come to learn as much from the way a patient looks at you as anything else. This man didn't know where he was, and he didn't know what had happened. He was still regaining consciousness, but his eyes were open and they were tracking objects. His pupils were reactive to light. He would be OK, even if he wasn't right then.

"You're going to be OK, soldier, you understand?"

The soldier stared up blankly, confused and unaware of what was happening.

"Sir?"

"You got hit by a rocket but you're going to be OK."

"Sir?"

"You're in Iraq, Jones[3]," I said, glancing through the shreds of uniform to find his name, "and you are going to be going back to America soon. You're going to be OK, so just relax as best as you can. We're going to be doing a lot of different things here but you're going to be fine."

"Is my dick OK?"

"Yes, it is. Your dick is just fine. In fact, everything is fine. You're going to be fine."

"OK, sir."

It never ceased to amaze me that every guy asked that question first. No matter how horrific a man's injuries are, the only thing he is able to focus on amidst the shock of the chaos is his penis. It was also amazing to me that the use of the word "sir" was literally a subconscious function. This guy didn't know where he was or what had happened to him. But if a soldier remembers anything when his life is at risk, it is to use the word "sir" when asking about the status of his penis.

John and our medics had fully prepped for the other casualties and the wave of trauma we were expecting. Over the

---

[3] Name modified for privacy

next several minutes it became apparent that the wave was not going to materialize. The other men in the tent had been killed instantly. Miraculously, for some inexplicable reason, there were only two other men in the tent at the time of the explosion. Had the normal number been in their cots, we would have lost a third of a platoon.

We turned our attention to securing a medevac for Jones, who was still shell-shocked. He had a shrapnel wound right next to his ear that was concerning. Although not immediately life threatening, it looked like it may have pierced his skull. We would find out weeks later that, in fact, he had a piece of metal lodged in his brain. He spent months recuperating from the blast at Walter Reed.

Jones left, and we all started to clean the aid station up and restock the supplies that had been opened. The adrenaline slowly wore off, and we were left to think quietly among ourselves in the hangover that remained. It was time for us to turn the grimmest aspect of war, and as usual none of us were in the mood to handle it. We had to clean up the scene at the tent and do our best to collect the remains for body bags.

My medics stepped forward and handled the hardest part of the job, and I am grateful to this day that they insulated me from dealing with the grim reality that is involved. After they had packed up the remains they were able to find, it was my job to go formally declare their deaths. We collected the remains into a trailer that I called the "death bin." It was little more than a nondescript metallic railcar trailer that sat outside our aid station. It was the final common pathway for any hero who died in our sector. I got to know that trailer all too well.

I walked into the trailer to declare the mechanism of death for the soldiers from the tent. As I opened the door, I saw the first body lying before me, severed in half. The soldier's heart and aorta were openly dangling from his thorax, lying just above a pile of intestines that were ruptured all over. The left ventricle of his heart was shredded into tufts of meat that lay there, dangling in a gruesome dance above the layers of feces that had been eviscerated from his bowels.

The other soldier's body had remained intact by and large, and it, too, lay in a lifeless pile a few feet away. I turned over the second body, and a gush of blood spilled out onto my hands from a massive hole that had ripped through his neck and upper thorax. His lung parenchyma could be seen lying there, still pink with blood oozing all around it. His face was obliterated. Shrapnel had torn off everything from his jaw to his forehead. The gelatin from his brains dripped out where eye sockets used to be. I was always relieved when I could see exposed gelatin. That way I could know for certain that my brother had been killed instantly before he could feel pain and suffering. Both soldiers lay lifeless in pools of blood, collected together into the anonymous black body bags.

[Images redacted for privacy]

For anyone who has witnessed death in its full, uncensored brutality, it is arguably the smell that sticks with you the longest. Entrails coated with stool admix with burned tissue and bodily fluids, and the haunting smell that results is one that can only be adequately described through firsthand experience. This was not my first trip into the death bin, and it would not be my last. But it was the first time I decided I had to write about it, so I would never forget what it meant to witness my brothers after their heroic lives were brought to an end:

The Death Bin

I suppose the title sounds ominous enough. As if it is meant for some kind of Hollywood production. It is pretty simple, really. The blue shipping freight trailer sits outside our aid station, and that's where we keep the bodies. The lifeless and cold lumps of humanity that lie in impossibly twisted contortions, their final agony blessedly done—but the evidence all too apparently remaining. Our men here train to no end. We have all acquired the most advanced medical knowledge and techniques known to man. And it only makes it all the more painful to realize we have nothing to offer when God's hand brings a life to an end.

I wish every leader in America had to spend a night in the death bin. One cold, frightening, infinitely lonely night. I don't doubt they have a rationale for their decisions. I don't doubt that some may even be genuine in intent. But I doubt any of them would have the stomach to lie next to a dead soldier and let him know that, despite his death, he is not alone. I know. I work in the death bin. Somehow, as if it is contagious, it is discomforting to be that close to death.

I'm sure the images I've seen will stay with me for the rest of my life. Not in a terrifying way, but, rather, with deep remorse that the poor souls I saw had nobody to help them when their young lives were cut tragically short. Perhaps war is inevitable.

Perhaps it is inherent to human nature. But somehow none of that is comforting. Because my men are dead, and nobody can explain why.

Why?

I say again. Why?

Why, motherfuckers, why?

Why does some poor family on the other side of the globe sleep peacefully right now, not knowing that tomorrow they will wake to the greatest tragedy of their lives? Why am I left to try to make rational decisions for that family about what to keep and what to simply throw away? Do you keep the wallet soaked in blood? Does that mean something to his family? It probably doesn't. They probably don't want to see it. But who am I to say? Can they ever know I tried with all of my heart to save their son? Will they ever know he didn't suffer? Will they, too, see that his heart is dangling outside of his thorax— exposed raw from the shrapnel that tore him in half? Will they ever know that he was the unlucky one, and that his other comrade somehow survived?

Yes, throw out the wallet but keep the contents. Clean the blood off them. Rinse the ID cards. Sterilize the awfulness that just unfolded here. Put a blanket over his cold body. This bin is chilly, and it is our job to keep him comfortable. That's what my family would want for me. This is our brother. He has already watched the guard and provided us the comfort of resting peacefully at night. Now it is our turn to watch guard over him. Watch guard over him now, so he, too, may rest peacefully forevermore.

CHAPTER 9
IAW CFR § 2635.802, J 2-303 WE'RE NOT TERRORISTS

"To reach…press one…IRS inquiries….press four….your call is important to us…"

The satellite phone crackled in and out as I tried to make a call to the IRS again. Iraqna phones, as they were called, worked about one out of forty tries and usually lasted for about three minutes before cutting out. The calling cards cost fifty cents a minute, charged upon initiation of a call whether it went through or not. Apparently satellite phones aren't real high on the priority list in a war zone.

John and I had continued to push to evacuate a child for reconstructive burn surgery, but we still couldn't get word about the legal forms that were required for the foundation to make it possible. We had already gone through multiple attempts with other candidates who weren't able to get a visa from the National Iraqi Assistance Center (NIAC), but we had finally found someone who was already connected enough to have gotten past the early stages of that hurdle. Now we were working on arranging the customs fees and transportation to convoy the child to safety. Unfortunately the primary contact in Kuwait at the Humanitarian Operations Center (HOC) was a dirty customs official who extorted bribes from anyone who tried to transport evacuees through his airport. He was on salary at the HOC that was run by the US and Kuwaiti governments. Yet there he was, the only gatekeeper for escape, attempting to extort bribes in order for kids to get medical care.

As active-duty officers, we had to be certain every penny that was associated with the project was transparently accounted for and fully audited by an independent third party. I had alerted the two US officers at the NIAC that their counterpart at the Kuwaiti HOC may very well be corrupted, but they never did anything about it. In their eyes, at least he wasn't as corrupted as the Iraqi Ministry of Health officials who were trying to kill us.

"Hello, my name is...your IRS representative today... recorded for quality assurance...How can I...?"

The Iraqna call, for a change, had apparently gone through.

"Sir, I'm calling from Iraq regarding our 501(c)3 nonprofit application."

"...sorry but the...let me transfer you..."

"NO! NO, WAIT!"

The line went dead. I'd lost track of how many times I'd repeated that same exercise in futility. Calling the IRS and the Treasury Department with a perfectly normal phone inside the United States was already frustrating enough. In Iraq, it was impossible.

I glanced through the letter we had received about various legal forms that were required for our foundation. Since we operated outside the United States, our application had to be routed through congressional offices and through the offices that managed international sanctions. I couldn't believe my eyes as I read through the materials they had sent us. As I sat and parsed through the legalese, I started to figure out what they were asking. *They refused to approve our nonprofit application until John and I could prove we weren't terrorists.* Hilarious! Two active-duty officers had to prove to our own government that we weren't terrorists!

Every time we filed a form with the international sanctions office, we had to have it blessed through military JAG (judge advocate general) lawyers to be certain we were adhering to active-duty regulations. Each correspondence with the JAG lawyer took a few days due to the nature of the communication lines and difficulties moving documents. None of those forms even touched on the forms that are required to procure a visa from the State Department. The legal hurdles involved were mind-boggling and, in reality, were harder to deal with than the rockets and roadside bombs.

Here is an example of one of hundreds of memorandums we completed in the process:

JONATHAN HEAVEY, M.D., BATTALION SURGEON

1ST BATTALION, 502D INFANTRY REGIMENT

101ST AIRBORNE DIVISION (AIR ASSAULT)

UNIT 6038 FOB JUSTICE

APO, AE 09378

REPLY TO ATTENTION OF:

AFZB-KB-G-SN   7 October 2008

MEMORANDUM OF RECORD

SUBJECT: Hope.MD, EIN 26-********, 501(c)3 application

TO: IRS, Attn: Janine L. ***** -7830; ID# 31-*****

Ms. *****,

Thank you for your consideration of our application for 501(c)3 tax-exempt nonprofit status. We appreciate the information you provided and look forward to maintaining full compliance with relevant statutes and guidelines. To help elucidate our administrative oversight and processes, I would offer the following replies to your inquiries:

1. Penalties of Perjury Declaration:

   As instructed, the Penalties of Perjury Declaration is signed and attached as the final page of this document.

2. Website Contents

   The hardcopy printouts of our website contents are included. Should you wish to access a registered account, you may do so using the username info@hope.md and the password ********. We included a printout of the single additional page that registered users can access, as the additional content is negligible.

3. Regulatory Compliance with OFAC, SDN, Treasury Department Statutes

   IAW 31 CFR § Part 596, our organization does not have any relationships, financial or otherwise, to any OFAC sanctioned states, individuals, or organizations. We noted the additional countries, including Iraq, that are at risk of harboring SDNs. We carefully reviewed the SDN database and have downloaded a copy for our organization records. IAW policy, Hope.MD will never "enter into a relationship with a grantee where any doubts exist about the grantee's ability to ensure safe delivery of charitable resources independent of influence by or association with any terrorist organization."

   Additionally, although we do not have any downstream grant recipients, we apply safeguards to our financial transactions to prevent exploitation by terrorists, terrorist organizations, and terrorist supporters. The vast majority of our purchases are from American-based corporations—such as airlines, hotels, and hospitals—that facilitate care for our patients. Our patients do not receive cash from the Foundation, and we only distribute funds pertaining to clinical cases to registered organizations that submit signed receipts on organization letterhead. Minor administrative transactions such as website design, copies, and other office expenses are tracked through our checking account with Bank of America (Routing **********: Acct *************).

   We carefully reviewed the US Treasury Department voluntary guidelines for charitable activities and will maintain compliance with their recommendations and guidelines.

4. Compliance with Revenue Ruling 63-252, 1963-2 C.B. 101 and 66-79, 1966-1 C.B. 48

A. Are contributions, gifts, and grants paid only to organizations exempt under IRC 501(c)(3)? If not, please explain the criteria that will be used to maintain expenditure responsibility. How will you ensure that the grants paid will be used for exempt purposes under IRC 501(c)(3)?

As noted in the regulation, most foreign entities are not registered under IRC 501(c)(3) and as such our transactions—particularly those involving the evacuation of children—will involve payments to non-registered entities.

By policy Hope.MD does not make expenditures to foreign individuals, only to registered organizations with the ability to accept electronic financial transactions at an institutional bank account. As an additional measure to maintain expenditure responsibility, Hope.MD will only grant reimbursement to foreign entities that provide signed receipts on organization letterhead, including organizational contact information.

Funds distributed to foreign organizations will be for the express purpose of evacuating children for charitable surgical care IAW IRC 501(c)(3) tax-exempt activities.

B. Safeguards to prevent diversion for non-exempt purposes.

• What kind of due diligence investigation is done in advance of selecting foreign-based organizations to benefit from your activities?

Hope.MD currently only operates in Iraq, and selects foreign-based organizations that are duly recognized by the Iraqi and US embassy for NGO/IGO activity. Should our operations expand to additional (non-OFAC) countries, we will undertake similar due diligence inquiries with local embassy officials to work through authorized NGO/IGO organizations. Should we be forced into functioning in an environment where official diplomatic structure is unclear due to war or other disaster, we will defer to US or UN identification of organizations acting in good faith humanitarian relief efforts.

• What provisions are used by the organization to ensure any assets used in carrying out its activities with foreign entities are used for their intended purpose?

As previously discussed, by policy Hope.MD does not make expenditures to foreign individuals, only to registered organizations with the ability to accept electronic financial transactions at an institutional bank account. As an additional measure to maintain accountability, Hope. MD will only grant reimbursement to foreign entities that provide signed receipts on organization letterhead, including organizational contact information.

• What reports or other mechanisms are used to track the use of assets?

All transactions are electronically recorded from our checking account with Bank of America. The organizations putting those funds to use all provide receipted reports for expenses they incurred during the evacuation of a child.

- If your organization makes or plans to make repeated grants to the same foreign grantee, or the same foreign grantee will benefit repeatedly from the organization's activities, how often does it perform renewed due diligence on the grantee?

  Hope.MD will not be making recurring grants. We review our list of participating organizations no less than annually to maintain regulatory compliance.

- Are, or will, grant agreements, reports, and other significant correspondence written or accurately translated into English? Are grant funds to be disbursed by check? By electronic funds transfer? By cash?

  Significant correspondences will be written in English, with translation in other languages only offered as a courtesy when available. No contractual arrangements will be performed in foreign language. Funds to foreign entities are distributed by electronic transfer to facilitate record-keeping. Cash, if used at all, is only authorized for minor office administrative duties such as making copies and sending faxes.

C. In the aftermath of September 11, 2001, what practices has your organization formed to ensure that foreign expenditures or grants are not diverted to support terrorism or other non-charitable activities? If you operate in a sanctioned country, will you acquire from OFAC the appropriate registration and license? When you conduct activities in Iraq and at a later date in other war-torn countries, will you check the OFAC list for names of persons with whom you are dealing who may reside in the sanctioned or non-sanctioned countries in which the organization may be operating?

   Hope.MD only works with foreign NGO/IGO organizations that are authorized diplomatic channels or entities that submit documented receipts on organization letterhead. We do not use cash with foreign entities, and we do not perform "advance" transactions that can be diverted. We only distribute funds after documented and qualifying expenses have been incurred.

   Should we expand to operations in a sanctioned country, we would file for an OFAC license and adhere to all regulatory standards. We will regularly review the OFAC listing of SDNs to avoid any transactions with such individuals and organizations. This includes SDNs residing in countries like Iraq that are not sanctioned but potentially harbor SDNs.

D. A domestic organization may not qualify for exemption if its primary activity is supporting a foreign government. Supporting a foreign government is not a recognized charitable purpose under IRC 501(c) (3). State whether or not your organization is directly supporting a foreign government.

Hope.MD does not support any foreign government.

As a required disclaimer, although I am an active duty officer, the Foundation is legally and fiscally autonomous. Therefore IAW CFR § 2635.802, J 2-303, it should not be construed to be condoned or endorsed by official US military policy.

POC for this memorandum is the undersigned at jonathan.heavey@ us.army.mil (phone and fax are unavailable in Baghdad).

Penalties of Perjury Declaration:

Under penalties of perjury, I declare that I have examined this information, including accompanying documents, and, to the best of my knowledge and belief, the information contains all relevant facts relating to the request for the information, and such facts are true, correct, and complete.

_____	7 October 2008
Jonathan Heavey, M.D.	Date

_____	_____
Rachel Gilliar, J.D., Director	Date

In accordance with Section 9.02(13)(b) of the Rev. Proc. 2008-4 this statement is signed by myself and Ms. Rachel Gilliar, J.D., who is a Board member and Director of Hope.MD. IAW the regulation, Ms. Gilliar is an officer whose duties 'extend beyond obtaining a letter or ruling of determination.' She votes in matters pertinent to the management of the Foundation.

I went through months and months of exchanges like this, and I was beyond neurotic about it since both John and I were active-duty officers. The legal implications for our careers were palpable at every step, so we made absolutely certain every penny was openly tracked with tax filings on our Web site.

Yet, in contrast to what we did, our civil affairs team ran around with suitcases full of cash that had virtually no regulatory strings attached. Hell, if they could find *anyone* interested in working on contracts, they would throw the money at him. The civil affairs embezzlement game became a favorite tactic for our enemies. Some local national would come play friendly on our base, perhaps offering to work as a translator or cook. They would find out who was on the civil affairs team and wait until they heard about the things civil affairs needed done in the sector. They would then put together a one-page handwritten write-up about the wonderful work they were prepared to do, et voila, they would get tens of thousands of dollars. After the cash got handed over to them, they would promptly disappear into the ether and use US taxpayer money to buy weapons to kill US soldiers. It was ridiculous! Did you ever hear the one about the ninety-six thousand M-16s that were somehow lost on the black market? That's how we roll—we give our enemies money to buy weapons to use to shoot at our own men!

Given all the complexity involved in coordinating funds, John and I decided we would just pay what we could out of pocket to evacuate the first child. It wasn't a huge sum of money, and if that had been the only limitation, we would have made it happen months earlier. As plans continued to come together for the first child to go to America, we also contacted a number of other humanitarian organizations to try to coordinate efforts for the future. We wrote to Unicef, the Gates Foundation, the Clinton Foundation, Save the Children, the International Red Cross, Calvert Investments, Project Hope, and numerous others. At every step of the way we expected some large humanitarian organization to step forward and say, "Don't worry guys, we already have this under control". We were just a couple of junior officers sitting in a dungeon. Certainly some group with more resources was mitigating this disaster, right? I mean, didn't we just see Angelina Jolie come through here in body armor? But time after time the response was the same: everyone had ceased operations in Iraq due to the violence.

It was quite a paradox, really. The people who were best suited to solve horrific problems were unable to function in an area because the problems were so horrific. Maybe that isn't a paradox. Maybe it is more like an oxymoron. Or irony. Whatever the hell it is, the tragic results are the same.

At one point we got responses from our own State Department Provincial Reconstruction Teams (PRTs) and the US Agency for International Development (USAID) teams. Their replies are still mind-boggling to me to this day. The PRT and USAID employees were mid-career professionals who, it turns out, function in teams of three to four people. A typical PRT was four guys. Four guys! Four guys make up a *provincial* reconstruction team? Invariably they would love the proposal we sent them, but in the same breath they would tell us how their funding guidelines precluded them from providing any support. Our project apparently didn't pertain to the items they were authorized to purchase, so they couldn't do anything with the multi-million-dollar budgets they wielded. The icing on the cake was that each team would end their reply by asking if *we* could help *them* evacuate dozens of kids that they knew who needed help. Sure thing, guys, no problem. John and I threw together five grand of our own money to make this happen, and you have a ten-million-dollar budget. Sure, we can help you. Let me pass around a tin cup the next time we're on patrol.

The exact same thing happened with Project Hope. Project Hope was tied directly to First Lady Bush and the White House. It had funding coming out of its ears for a children's hospital it spent seven years trying to build in Basra. The local populace knew this, and tragically there would be targeted bombings at the hospital. When I asked them if we could work together to evacuate a child, they thought it was a great idea. Then they sent me information on a bunch of kids they couldn't help and asked me if I could do anything. Sure, no problem, guys.

I know a surgeon who has volunteered to help for free and a family who has agreed to take in the child and guardian. Any chance you have a couple hundred bucks you could chip in for the plane ticket? Crickets…crickets.

Years later, I would have a meeting with a senior USAID leader who was in charge of President Obama's new global engagement directive. Sitting over coffee, surrounded by the immaculate corridors of the Reagan international trade building, I told him how the highly funded PRT and USAID teams had turned to us for help, rather than vice versa. Our group of state department officers and military officers had a common interest in a humanitarian project. We were all trying to do the same thing, and they even had children already screened and identified in their sectors. So what could possibly keep us from working with their department, or their department from working with us? Every step had been blessed by a lawyer and every penny was tracked openly with absolutely full accountability. They were literally sitting on hundreds of millions of dollars of reconstruction funds. They had run into incredible difficulty with graft and corruption when they tried to channel the funding through the Iraqi Ministry of Health. I understood that their policy processes set strict parameters on the uses for their capital. Rather than investing in cash and equipment that would inevitably be corrupted, why not invest in human capital that could not be corrupted and would pay a far greater dividend? All that we needed was help getting plane tickets for the children they had identified. Is it really that hard to buy a couple more plane tickets?

The senior USAID official I was meeting with nodded his head in total agreement, knowing exactly what I was driving at even before I had completed my rant. "Jon," he said, "many bureaucrats in DC refer to this phenomenon as 'stove-piping,' where funds from one agency can't be authorized for use in another agency even when you have a clearly compelling problem that impacts both agencies." I sat listening, realizing that stove-piping was the pleasant way to say that nobody could give a shit about fixing problems that weren't specifically tasked to them from senior levels of command in their own agency. It was basically the American version of en shallah.

"We at USAID have been aware of stove-piping for years. It is so frustrating we've chosen to adopt a new terminology for it. We now prefer to call it 'a cylinder of excellence,' and it doesn't change a goddamn thing." We both laughed out loud at his new phrase—it captured everything so perfectly. Cylinders of excellence. Cylinders of excellence, indeed.

CHAPTER 10
SHITHOUSE IN SHULLA

I don't remember where I was when Kagger and Johnson[4] got hit, but I remember knowing once again that the blast was so close it must have killed someone. The chaos was instantaneous, almost routine in its predictability.

"WHERE THE FUCK WAS IT?!"

Sprinting and scrambling, we clawed to get inside a hardened shelter by the aid station. The blast had concussed through my ears, triggering my senses and making it obvious the kill zone had come knocking once again.

"FUCKING GRID…GET THE FUCKING GRID!"

"ROCKETS—FUCK—ROCKETS!"

The wicked hiss of indiscriminant death screamed through the sky, too fast to flinch.

"TAMPA, ON…TAMPA, THREE DOWN COMING IN HOT!"

"NO CUBS—CUBS NORTH RIGHT AT THE FUCKING GATE!"

"DOC, DOC, FUCKIN' EFP HIT RIGHT AT THE GATE…DOC, RIGHT AT THE FUCKING GATE!!"

---

[4] Names modified for privacy

"WE NEED MORE FUCKING MEDICS! WE NEED MORE FUCKING MEDICS!!"

I think our platoon sergeant, Staff Sergeant Logan, was the first man to get there. Or it might have been our scout medic, Corporal Price-Picon. I don't know, as much as I wish I could say. They responded within seconds. I don't know how either of them managed to move themselves directly into that vortex of shit. I was shaking violently again, trying my best to breathe myself down from believing I was just about to die.

Within minutes, two casualties were upon us, and this time it was obvious that they had huge problems. Kagger's leg lay shredded in a pile of meat, bleeding profusely onto everything around him. He was screaming in agony, confused, and in an altered state of mind. He was critically wounded and was clearly in hemorrhagic shock. Contrary to what you see in the movies, mortally wounded people don't lie and talk movingly about their loved ones. They often try to punch objects around them in the midst of their chaos and confusion, and they typically scream in agony. They become violent by reflex without any cognitive functions intact. Kagger was past the point of asking about his dick. He was one step short of death.

Someone had managed to tourniquet his leg already, which saved his life. He was bleeding enough as it was. Had his torn artery continued to bleed unabated, he would have bled to death and exsanguinated in less than a minute.

I stood back, largely just getting in the way of my medics, who were already on top of the situation. I could see how other PROFIS docs would be a terrible burden for medics to deal with if they interfered. Even as a trauma-trained doc, I was so shell-shocked I didn't know if I could be of any use. Thankfully, as we say in emergency medicine, Kagger's screams were music to my ears. They are the "beautiful sound of a patent airway," so he didn't need to go through a complex process to get an emergency breathing tube. I tried to focus and walk myself through what needed to be done at that point, since his airway was open and his bleeding had been slowed.

I reached for our special blood clotting agent called hemcon chitosan to help stop the bleeding that was forcing its way through Kagger's tourniquet. The gaping wound in his leg was still spurting and oozing large amounts of blood despite the tourniquet, and I had to probe through his flesh to try to find the artery. Kagger, already beside himself in agony, screamed as my fingers probed his gaping tissues. His screams helped cover the grotesque sound of raw tissue being violated as my fingers penetrated his muscle layers. The blood and tissue were both slick and sticky, causing everything to squish in place like a bowl full of writhing larvae. Once I found the artery, I packed the chitosan over it deep inside the wounds while another medic, Sergeant Avery, secured it in place. Kagger's bleeding stopped, and his vitals began to stabilize. Another medic, Staff Sergeant Mullen already had morphine out and ready to help Kagger cope with the excruciating pain from his injuries.

While I had my nose in Kagger's wounds, John had already coordinated with medics and handled everything on the other casualty on the other side of the room. He was so professional, I always just looked at what he did in total awe. He had already given the other soldier morphine and a special IV medication called hespan. The hespan is an intravascular volume replacement that acts as a kind of artificial blood without the risk of a full transfusion. It helps the circulating blood re-perfuse damaged organs, and the soldier John had treated was already clearly getting better. He, too, was out of the woods for a breathing tube, as John had assessed his pulse oximeter and other measures to be sure the soldier's lungs had been spared in the blast.

We continued to package the two casualties and a medevac was arranged. There was the typical drama as our medevac liaison wanted more information than we had and demanded not to wait longer than thirty seconds in our landing zone due to the ongoing gunfire and mortars. If I was a PROFIS prima donna, the medevac officers from the Green Zone were the genuine debutantes. We told them what we could, and they grumbled at us as usual. But in no short order Kagger and Johnson were on a bird and headed to the OR.

Two years later I was working the night shift at Walter Reed, halfway exhausted, when a young man in tennis shoes and shorts walked with a limp into my ER. He sat down and patiently waited to be seen. As I scanned over the chart, absentmindedly flipping through another routine encounter, I noticed he had old injuries on his leg that looked oddly familiar. They were the same wounds I had packed with hemostatic chitosan two years prior on the opposite side of the globe.

I hadn't recognized Kagger without the blood and chaos that was part of our last encounter, and he had no idea who I was since he had been wounded so severely. I turned and asked him, "Were you with the Deuce in Iraq?" He nodded in agreement. "Did you get hit by an EFP right at the gate for FOB Justice?" He looked at me, a bit confused, and again nodded. "I think I was the doctor who packed your leg." Two years later, and half a world away from the hellhole we once shared, I got to shake Kagger's hand for the first time. Someone grabbed a camera phone and snapped a picture of the two of us, and to this day it remains as the highlight of my medical career.

* * *

Shortly after Kagger got hit by the EFP, our unit started to expand operations into yet another proverbial slum of Baghdad known as Shulla. I always found the term "Baghdad slum" to be an obvious redundancy, but no media report would be complete without it, I guess. Shulla was a Shiite-dominant part of town that JAM fighters from Sadr City were using as a hideout area. They had concocted a new weapon we called an IRAM, which allowed them to lob munitions off the back of a moving bongo truck. Bongo trucks were the universally dilapidated pickups that everyone drove around town. They usually had flimsy wooden side rails and some kind of canvas cover over the back, and these helped hide the tubes they used to lob rockets onto our bases. One bongo truck might be transporting melons or fruit to the market. The next would be a mobile rocket pad, and nobody could tell the difference until it was too late.

The first IRAM strike had decimated our men at the joint security station (JSS) right down the road. Our PTDS overhead blimp camera caught footage from the attack, and we all watched in horror as one huge explosion after another pounded directly into the heart of the JSS.

We could feel the reverberations growling menacingly under our feet as the attack unfolded just a few clicks away. For some reason we never did treat any overflow casualties from the IRAM hit, but the unceasing series of explosions could be felt for miles all around. I can't describe the feeling you have in the pit of your stomach when you feel the distant, but distinct, ground-shaking tremor that the bombs create. I do not know how many men we lost that day, but judging from what we saw, I can only imagine. I caught a snapshot off the video feed so I could remember just how powerful the IRAM's destruction had been.

In the photo you can see a white shuttle bus and a large MRAP armored vehicle (off to the left). The blast walls surrounding the base and the guard tower are about thirty feet tall. The billowing smoke came up as round after round of mortars directly impacted the base. At the end of the mortaring, the truck that was carrying the rounds smashed into the gate and detonated hundreds of pounds of explosives.

The threat from the IRAM quickly became the top priority for our commanders. They initiated a series of operations designed to cordon off the cells of militants in Shulla whom they thought were responsible for the new bombing technique. Within a few days, the battalion was spun up and we were moving men out onto new streets, putting up blast walls and IRAM bars that prevented bongo trucks from driving nearby.

I packed my things into the back of a Humvee late one night and bounced around in the lunar landscape for a few hours to get to the forward security station where our operations would be started. We rolled out on the convoy during the night across patches of roads and moonscape. All I could see was dust, and I didn't have a headset, so I just sat and waited for the team to figure out where we were going. Being a type-A control freak, I always found that to be disconcerting. I like to know where I am, as if somehow that helps minimize the risk of being killed. I had studied Arabic for what seemed like months, but I hadn't been able to master any of it. I had memorized one phrase, though, in case we ever got lost in a convoy like the one we were in that night. *"Mid-fudluck, ana tabeeb-waji fee alum. May-a-jib-nee George Bush. Karib-La,"* or "Please, I'm a doctor and can help you. I don't like George Bush—*fuck him.*"

Our convoy pulled into an old warehouse somewhere in the middle of the night and called it quits. I unloaded my stuff and looked around for a place to crash. I kicked through the layers of pigeon shit with my boot to scrape a patch of concrete bare for a bed. A couple hours later, the sun was up and the heat woke me. We had made it to our JSS with Bravo Company, where our medics, Sergeant Panduro, Sergeant Shanklin, Sergeant Beaubien, and Sergeant Parker, worked. Actually, I'm not sure if anyone knew what Sergeant Parker's real rank was but it didn't matter. Whatever his rank, he was a funny-ass Cajun redneck from the swamps of Louisiana who kept us all laughing, all the time. He had gotten pulled out of civilian life as a stop-loss deployment, but he managed to keep his sense of humor all the same—even if he was living in a decrepit warehouse full of pigeon shit.

Sergeant Beaubien and Sergeant Shanklin were two NCOs with outsized muscles and rugged good looks—all of which won them the nickname of "the ambiguously gay duo." The beautiful girlfriends they paraded around in America looked like a thinly veiled guise of an excuse to hide their true love for each other. And Sergeant Panduro, well, Sergeant Panduro was the fastest five-foot-nothing guy you've ever met, who, like me, never met a chalupa he didn't like. He was the ringleader of the group and a hell of a good medic. They had put these guys out with Bravo Company because they were our best medics. Our commanders had figured that Bravo Company would see the worst of the worst, and so far they had been right.

As I unloaded my rucksack and got settled in, Panduro told me about how they had evacuated a mutual friend of ours, Lieutenant Luckett, in a blast shortly before our arrival. Luckett was an impossibly sharp guy, and one of the up-and-coming leaders of the unit. Every guy in the unit hated him because he was undeniably the best all-American guy you could ever meet. The jerk didn't have the decency to leave any good material from the gene pool for the rest of us. Tragically, his Humvee got destroyed by an EFP, and he lost his leg and portions of his other foot in the blast. A Reuter's photographer snapped a photograph of the scene as the medevac bird landed, and Lieutenant Luckett—as only Luckett could do—gave a thumbs-up as his legs were still oozing with blood.

Panduro and his medics had done everything right and saved Luckett's life. They salvaged what they could of his limbs, and we got updates about Luckett as he rehabbed for an extended period at Walter Reed. He was still there when I returned later that year, exercising like an Olympic athlete in the same amputation ward where Kagger had also managed to regain the use of his leg. Within two years Luckett returned to battle again despite missing a leg and several toes. The mountains of Afghanistan were no match for his heroic spirit.

As I got settled into the routine in Shulla, the days seemed to pass incredibly slowly, though the time with the Bravo Company medics was always entertaining. Our meals were often MREs or tuna packets we could scrape up from care packages. One night we sat talking in a circle like stupid teenage kids, just fantasizing about what we would have in our dream refrigerator or dream pantry back home. Parker was particularly gifted at the dream kitchen game. One night he started talking about nachos, and that was pretty much all she wrote. Endless nachos at Beningans. Man, what a treat. Piled high with jalapenos and crappy meat, sour cream, and salsa oozing into the chips until they were soggy. It sounded so good I just couldn't wait to get back to America to eat them. We were all hollering about crappy nachos from Beningans like they were the greatest fucking thing on earth. In that tiny shithole corner of the world, anything about America was the greatest fucking thing on earth.

Within a few days of our tactical operations, we had several hundred men staged in two warehouses waiting for further orders. The warehouses we were in had old corrugated tin roofs that wouldn't have stopped a baseball from crashing through, let alone a mortar round. As the only doctor there, it was a bit unnerving for me to think just how screwed we would have been if a mortar round hit the warehouse.

One night, one of our interpreters disappeared, which was rarely—no, actually, *never*—a good sign. It usually meant the terp had defected back to the other side and was feeding information on our operations to the people who were trying to kill us. On the night our terp disappeared, we watched a security video that showed a small white bongo truck pull up with IRAM explosives into a neighborhood near our base. We watched as the men in the truck pointed in different directions. They drove off slowly, and within ten minutes we felt the reverberations from repeated blasts that pounded the main Iraqi Army checkpoint in Shulla. Checkpoint twenty, as we called it, was our primary checkpoint in our sector for the operations we were starting. We had been late in starting the operation, though, so we were still in the warehouses back up the road.

Later that night our first sergeant found a note on his bed from the interpreter. "First Sergeant—got a call we might be bombed. Have to run." I didn't know whether to laugh or cry at the absurdity of it. At least he was courteous enough to leave a note to tell us when we were about to get killed! Thankfully, he fed the wrong fucking information to his dirty partners in crime.

The next day we rolled out to checkpoint twenty to set up our forward aid station for the operation. I had thought that Saddam's dungeon was a suboptimal setting to live in, but when I got to checkpoint twenty, I realized just how luxurious the dungeon had been. Checkpoint twenty was literally a shithole. The Iraqis didn't typically use toilets to defecate in; they simply dug a hole in the ground with some runoff that they used as their toilet/shower/kitchen sink. Checkpoint twenty was a burned-out old mosque with one such hole and little more. The mosque windows were all blasted out, and the walls were charred and crumbling to the ground. The roof was collapsed in different portions, with the remaining portions looking as though they were trying desperately to appease gravity. The desert dirt flowed throughout, and by the communal shithole, the feces and urine admixed with the dirt. Together they made an impossibly slippery and disgusting paste-like substance that had spread around everywhere.

The Iraqi Army (IA) soldiers were scattered around the place, lying on lice-infested mattresses that were soaked in the stool-paste. They lounged around with one another in oddly effeminate manners, slapping each other on the ass and acting completely bizarrely. They lay there like animals in a jungle, lounging around the cesspool in the fetid environment.

I looked around at the rooftops, again looking for angles that a sniper could use on us. The walls were so porous—including one that had fallen down completely—it was impossible to find a place that wasn't in the line of sight of another crumbled structure. The damage from the IRAM blast the day before was visible all around, with craters in the earth around the mosque and portions of the "building" that had clearly just been destroyed. With so much character to offer, both Staff Sergeant Logan and I agreed it was a perfect spot to set up our aid station.

I got the trauma supplies that I could ready to go and sat back praying that nobody would be stupid enough to engage our men during the operation. As I opened my medical supply crates, the Iraqi Army slime bags got off their mattresses and came crowding over to me. I had not anticipated their reaction to the medical supplies, and before I knew it, I was surrounded by a mob of filthy foreign soldiers carrying weapons carelessly and shouting out, "Mistah, mistah!" They gestured with their feces-coated hands about things they wanted medicine to fix, and they were sloppy enough to "flash" their muzzles in uncontrolled directions in their desperation. As the mob slowly surrounded me, I was becoming intensely uncomfortable, as there was no control whatsoever over who was doing what. It felt like a herd of desperate animals was descending on me, and I didn't like it one bit.

As I felt the crowd of IA soldiers closing in, I was bracing myself to start swinging. Thankfully, Sergeant Logan sensed my discomfort, and he had no qualms about playing enforcer. An intimidating NCO if you ever met one, Sergeant Logan let loose at the top of his lungs, "BACK THE FUCK UP, YOU HAJI MOTHERFUCKERS!" The IA soldiers got the point, and quickly. It was incredible to see the parallels to the animal world. Nobody could speak each other's language, but I clearly had something all the animals wanted. Equally clearly, Sergeant Logan was the alpha dog who set the rules. Words can't describe how relieved I was to have the alpha dog on my side.

The night started to set in and we sat listening to gunfire popping off in the distance. Like firecrackers on the Fourth of July, it had become an unremarkable part of the daily routine. As the sun set, Sergeant Logan introduced me to a guy named Sergeant Wolfe, who had done four prior tours and was the most decorated veteran anyone knew. Sergeant First Class Wolfe had a silver star with a valor device—an incredibly unusual combination that spoke volumes about what he had done and witnessed in the war. Wolfe was a natural-born leader. He was confident yet humble in everything he did, and he always managed to get shit done. Period.

I sat up and talked with Sergeant Wolfe for a couple of hours, and I was fascinated by what he had to say about the war and our national politics. I felt like a student listening in awe to a world-class teacher. Even though I was sitting there with him in the middle of a combat operation, he had seen and known so much more than me it was mind-boggling to think about the kinds of sacrifices he had made. I would never want to put words in his mouth, so I will keep the lessons he taught me to myself. But suffice it to say, killing and fighting change men in many ways that civilians will never be able to appreciate—no matter how hard they may try.

Our operations dragged through the night, and the fighting never got closer than a few clicks away in the distance. Eventually the gunfire was so random that I just ignored it and lost interest. We were apparently the more effective force in the battle, so I started to doze off. I was pretty content to be bored. We weren't going to get any warning about casualties anyway, and it was supposed to be the Iraqi Army units that were leading the charge by that point in the operation. I fell asleep sitting on the concrete, with my nose balanced on my body armor.

A few hours later, Sergeant Wolfe woke me to tell me we were done at checkpoint twenty. I always thought the Rambo-style PTSD-flashback stereotype was a bunch of bullshit. But when Sergeant Wolfe woke me up, I was instantly startled and confused in the middle of a hellhole mosque in the dark. I grabbed Sergeant Wolfe instinctively, thinking he was trying to kill me. I had his body armor by the neck collar but in my confusion I couldn't understand why his skin looked white in the moonlight. I had pulled my fist back to punch him when I realized he was yelling in English, "DOC! DOC!! DOC, IT'S ME!!!!" Two other guys, Sergeant Logan and our first sergeant, saw what happened and were stepping in to intervene. Within a few seconds I started to realize where I was and we all just burst out laughing. It probably sounds really stupid now, but I hadn't laughed that hard in a long, long time. Thankfully Sergeant Wolfe didn't just opt to kill me on the spot.

We wrapped up the operation for the night and took another convoy through the moonscape dirt to get back to the warehouse at Shulla. I felt like I had shit-paste all over me, but we finally had some baby wipes to get cleaner than we had been before. I fell asleep for the night, looking forward to stripping down and pouring a bottle of water over my head in the morning for a truly luxurious shower.

CHAPTER 11
STARFISH HAS LANDED

While I was in Shulla, John Knight was in the dungeon on FOB Justice. He had kept on working to evacuate a child for surgery, but we had not been able to overcome the legal hurdles and other challenges involved. John and I had asked our local Iraqi doctor, Dr. K, to help us identify some children who would benefit from reconstructive burn surgeries or other trauma surgeries. Dr. K ran the risk of exposing himself as an American sympathizer in his community every time he wrote up a case report for us to review. Physicians in the local communities were often loyal to JAM, and invariably they would have suspicions about why Dr. K was asking questions about local children. The level of distrust on all sides was palpable and, sadly, something that we never could really overcome.

Before I left for Shulla, Dr. K had already identified a handful of cases for John and me to consider, but getting the logistics to align was incredibly challenging. We would sort through cases to find children who were stable enough to be evacuated, but they would have different clinical conditions that would require us to find new surgeons in America for each case. If we managed to create a clinical match, we would then need to find a host family in the area who would be willing to open their home to the child and a guardian. We reached that point on several occasions, but then the Iraqi family would become uncomfortable with the American combat vehicles parking near their home. On more than one occasion we got through the entire match process only to have the family disappear. Each step had to happen through the satellite connection, and the weather had to cooperate. Taken altogether, it felt like we were walking through waist-high molasses trying to get just one case coordinated.

I remember one case in particular that still haunts me to this day. We managed to find a match with a surgeon at the University of Virginia to perform heart surgery for a child named Ahmed. Ahmed was healthy enough to fly out of country without active medical treatment en route when we first started to evaluate his condition. I asked our combat support hospital if they could perform an ultrasound on Ahmed's heart to see if we could send the University of Virginia surgeon some basic information about his condition. I sent out e-mail requests in batches over the course of a few hours every day. Day by day, I slowly worked my way up through the chain of command at the combat support hospital—all the way up to the full bird colonel who ran it—trying to find a way for an ultrasound to be done on Ahmed's heart.

The full bird colonel indicated he couldn't do the study, but he put me back in touch with people on his staff whom I had already asked to do the study. The staff physicians were amenable to doing it once their boss had heard about our request, but of course I hadn't won any favors by going over their heads to find help with the issue. The staff physicians then told me the machine that they needed to use was out of order.

I figured out how to contact the technologist who managed the machine and he indicated it worked fine. Apparently it just didn't have any CDs to record the ultrasound images.

I contacted the staff physicians again and offered to buy a dozen CDs to have them shipped directly to the combat support hospital, along with a six-pack of beer for all their help. I never heard back from anyone again. I was clearly pushing uphill trying to call in favors from people who, quite frankly, just didn't give a shit. It wasn't their problem. It hadn't been "tasked" to them on a direct order from their chain of command. It wasn't part of their medical rules of engagement.

It seemed that wherever we went, we ran into excuse after excuse about MEDROE. MEDROE became the universal reflex that senior officers at the combat support hospital would use to avoid work or dodge a request from subordinates. While the "stove-piping" restrictions prevented us from working across federal agencies, MEDROE were used as an excuse to keep us from working up through senior levels within our own agency.

Now, don't get me wrong; nobody was doing anything maliciously or with purposeful intent to harm a child. But at the end of the day, evacuating a child for surgery was not specifically documented as part of our established MEDROE. I would come across a glimmer of hope here and an encouraging word there, but my requests didn't fall into anyone's lane of responsibility. My immediate supervisor was incredibly supportive and went out of his way to help, but he in turn was working uphill to find solutions to the challenges we faced in sector.

It never failed to amaze me how many of my colleagues in medicine were not concerned that the MEDROE created potentially profound conflicts with the Hippocratic oath. The Hippocratic oath is a professional oath that all physicians take to swear loyalty to patients who are brought to them for care. If you cite MEDROE as a reason you can't help a patient, you may not be actively harming them, but you sure as hell are walking into an ethical gray zone that doesn't fit with our moral obligations as physicians—much less as Americans.

Technically, the MEDROE allowed physicians to intervene and treat Iraqis in the event that "acute life, limb, or eyesight" were threatened. Functionally, this almost never happened because we didn't even have pediatric equipment at our forward trauma outposts. In Ahmed's case, his studies were not considered to be part of an acute threat to his life, limb, or eyesight. Although he was slowly going into heart failure due to his condition, it wasn't an acute event that fit within established MEDROE policies.

Ahmed slowly deteriorated by the day. I could not visit him or be involved in his care without compromising his safety, so I had to rely on periodic updates from Dr. K. Eventually Ahmed's condition became so acute that one of the surgeons we spoke with was willing to do the surgery even if we couldn't obtain an ultrasound prior to evacuation. Given the urgency of the situation, we just focused our energy on accelerating the visa clearance to get the legal paperwork in place.

In order to get the visa cleared, we started back into the series of exchanges with the Treasury Department that we had to file in order to prove we weren't terrorists. We managed to satisfy those requirements and the OFAC and FINCEN international sanctions restrictions. After we filed those forms, we had to obtain clearance from the JAG lawyers to accept funds for our foundation before the formal nonprofit 501(c)3 charter was approved by the IRS. I reached out to congressional offices in my home state to ask for help accelerating the 501(c)3 nonprofit charter, and I filed various inquiry forms with them. I wrote up letters and e-mails that the office used for an expedited charter, which ultimately did go through. Unfortunately the expedited charter accelerated the process from one year to six months, which was beyond the time we had available to evacuate Ahmed.

Eventually when I explained the situation to the JAG lawyers, they indicated we could accept funds even without the 501(c)3 charter, so we started to file the DS-156 paperwork that is required for the State Department embassy clearance. The DS-156 form is one of three forms that they required, and they also required a visit in person to the embassy in the Green Zone. I asked Dr. K if this was possible, but apparently it was not safe for Ahmed's family to be seen entering or leaving the Green Zone. I found a person from the State Department who worked in the consular section of the embassy and tried several dozen times over the course of a week to get through on the broken phone lines. Eventually I got a hold of him and I pleaded my case for Ahmed. He agreed to process the DS-156 on Ahmed's behalf and helped me work around the problems they had traveling to the Green Zone.

Unfortunately, I never had the opportunity to meet Ahmed or any of the other children that Dr. K had identified. It was too dangerous to risk meeting in person since the MRAP combat vehicles would send a signal to the neighborhood that Americans had visited. But Dr. K was always looking out for new cases, and he would develop patient reports on a regular basis for us to evaluate. Like a never-ending Rolodex, he would screen cases and keep bringing in files until all the stars could align for the right child.

One morning, while we were waiting for the legal clearances we needed to evacuate Ahmed, I saw Dr. K sitting in our aid station. I could tell by the look on his face that he wasn't his usual self.

We exchanged our normal greeting: *"Sabbah-al-jrear Sidi, kafa hal-uk?"* (Good morning, sir, how are you?) I followed up with my usual reply: *"Al-ham-du-lilla, wa-anta?"* (Good, by the grace of God, and you?) Dr. K just glanced down with a look that I had come to know all too often. He was despondent. He then proceeded to tell me what was on his mind. "Hey, Doc, I wanted to let you know. Ahmed died last night. Thank you for trying. He is in a better place now, en shallah."

I felt like I had been punched in the chest.

En shallah was right.

En shallah, en shallah, en shallah that whole fucking place. During the months of bullshit paperwork and logistical delays, Ahmed had died. Not because we couldn't help him. Not because he didn't deserve the help. Not because the surgery cost too much. Not because of anything but fucking bullshit piled on top of bureaucratic bullshit. En shallah was right.

I sat and drank my morning coffee, staring in disbelief and wondering how such a simple and obvious solution had failed yet again. A child had died because we couldn't file forms fast enough. Someone's son had the promise of American help within his grasp, and we fucking punted it. We fucking punted it.

It felt like I was a hamster on a wheel, always trying to pull the pieces together to get a child evacuated and never quite getting there. John felt the same way, and if it weren't for our friendship, I'm sure we would have failed in our mission and given up on the project long ago. After Ahmed died, we spent a lot of time just lifting weights and blowing off steam, trying not to think about how many times we had tried and failed to evacuate even a single child.

* * *

When I initially contacted the staff at the combat support hospital to ask for help with Ahmed, I exchanged some e-mails with a friendly pediatrician, Major H[5]. Major H had been willing to help us out, and it turned out that he, too, had been working to evacuate children with complex problems he came across. He had encountered the same problems with the MEDROE, and we had tried to finds ways we could help each other out. John and I were basically in a holding pattern after Ahmed's death. But while I was out on the operations in Shulla, Major H had kept working to find a way to evacuate children he knew at the combat support hospital. Eventually he contacted me to ask about a child he had identified named Rafal, who needed to be evacuated.

We had continued to exchange messages with him through the satellite, starting once again in an effort to find a clinical match with our surgeons back home. The night after I returned from checkpoint twenty, I got some significant news from John. We had a clinical match for Rafal, and, even better yet, his paperwork at the embassy had been cleared faster, thanks to Major H's efforts. Apparently he was close enough to the NIAC that he could work through their office to obtain a passport and visa.

Rafal had severe burn contractures that kept him from using his arms. Contractures are a type of scar tissue that

---

[5] Name modified for privacy

develops after full thickness burns cause the normal skin to slough off. Rafal had contractures that scarred his former arms into painfully contorted partial limbs that he could not use, and, worse yet, he had a life-threatening infection in the scar tissue. Burned skin loses its natural protection from bacteria that we all have on our skin, and in Rafal's case he had become infected with a deadly multi-drug-resistant bacteria known as methicillin resistant staph-aureus (MRSA).

Rafal would likely have died from the infection, and he already had lost the use of his hands due to the burns. Unfortunately, by MEDROE policy, he could not go on receiving care from the combat support hospital. They had already gone to great lengths to help him survive the acute phases of his burns, but they had to prepare to discharge him due to the MEDROE-related restrictions.

Nobody seemed to have any other option for helping him, so we all pitched in for his plane ticket and started working on the arrangements to evacuate him out of Iraq. Thankfully, since the NIAC and Major H had already found a way to obtain his passport, we had a head start on most of the remaining paperwork hurdles.

One tricky issue that we had never encountered before was that we had to find a non-pregnant female guardian to accompany Rafal on his trip to America. No men were allowed out of Iraq, and any woman who went with Rafal had to find a way to document the results of a pregnancy test. What would seem like a comically simple issue to address in America was actually a major challenge in theater. It wasn't like we could just drive up to a drugstore and buy a five-dollar pregnancy test. Rafal's grandmother was going to be his guardian, and even though she was obviously post-menopausal, she had to find a way to drive to the Green Zone and pay for a doctor's visit for a pregnancy test. To this day I am not sure how that happened; all I know is that it took quite a bit of time for it to be resolved.

Eventually, through a combination of efforts with John, Major H, and several charitable organizations, we were able to work through all the remaining legal issues to finalize his visa clearance. Rafal and his "non-pregnant female guardian" safely made their way down to Kuwait to the Humanitarian Operations Center. John and I paid a small fortune to gain clearance from the corrupted customs official there, and within a few days Rafal was on a flight on United Airlines on his way to the Shriner's Children's Hospital in Cincinnati.

Wow. Yes, wow. What a relief! When Rafal was finally settled with the host family and receiving his care, I thought that John and I should have our own little celebration. We had finally found a way to get our first starfish back into the ocean! It was incredibly exciting to think we had finally managed to accomplish what we had set out to do eight months earlier. We didn't have any alcohol allowed in theater, but we did find a way to have some nonalcoholic "near-beer" to celebrate. It felt like the weight of the world had been lifted off our shoulders. It didn't matter how many times we had tried and failed. We had finally nudged the boulder. We had finally trudged out of the quicksand. We had finally achieved the first step in what we had set out to do.

* * *

In the process of getting Rafal's visa processed, John and I came across a group called the Iraqi Children's Medical Initiative (ICMI) that was being spearheaded by a retired general. ICMI had been trying to coordinate some charitable relief efforts, although they functioned largely in the United States and didn't have any assets in theater. Like us, they were scraping together anything they could to help the situation.

A short time after Rafal was evacuated, one of the ICMI coordinators told me they had an opportunity to help a surgeon from Johns Hopkins operate on ten children at one time during a medical relief trip to Turkey. We also received an open commitment from James Wright, a former marine and the president of Dartmouth College, to help a child with surgery at the Dartmouth Hitchcock Medical Center. President Wright personally sent messages to a variety of leaders on campus to help our little project. Taken together, the two openings represented an incredible opportunity to ramp up what we had started with Rafal, and it was inspiring to think that the foundation we had hoped to build was starting to come to fruition. We had proven we could do it with our first starfish, and now in just a short time we had a large number of new cases taking shape.

Although I had not been able to procure grant support for what we were doing, both John and I were committed to funding things as long as necessary to keep the project moving forward. It felt like we had lifted this enormous mass to get Rafal evacuated—we had finally overcome the institutional inertia that had so tragically led to Ahmed's death. And now that Rafal had made it to America, we had the smallest ember of hope that we were desperately encouraging to grow. We used the satellite connection to contact numerous friends and family members, and with their donations, we continued to build on what had been done so far.

Unfortunately, despite the generosity from our family and friends, we were short of funding for the next ten children that ICMI had lined up to help with the surgeon from Johns Hopkins. I was convinced there had to be federal resources available for such an important issue, but I didn't know how to find anything to help us.

One night I set the satellite connection up to download a 242-page file from the Pentagon called FM 3-24. FM 3-24 is better known as the Army counterinsurgency manual, and to prove I was a glutton for punishment, I decided I was going to read the entire thing page by page. I sat down for a few days with a dedicated coffee shrine like I used to use during medical school, and thanks to the help of sacrificial offerings to the gods of caffeine, I made my way through all of the acronym-dense material. In the process I searched for any information that the senior combatant commanders had provided about funding for relief efforts or interagency cooperation with other federal entities.

One day I came across a section in the manual that mentioned a program called the commanders emergency response program (CERP). CERP gave local commanders the leeway to fund relief efforts in their sector, and it was designed to create the greatest institutional flexibility for local leadership. In fact, it was designed to break through the institutional "stove-piping" that prevented the provincial reconstruction teams and USAID teams from supporting our efforts. Although the PRT and USAID teams weren't allowed to contribute their funds to help the project, the new CERP program looked like the perfect way to build a collaborative effort with them. It was supposed to be the way that agencies could "play nice" with one another so local military commanders could act quickly and decisively on pressing humanitarian issues in their sector.

I drafted a formal CERP application, excitedly thinking we were going to be able to help ten children obtain surgery all at once. The surgeon from John Hopkins, Esen Akpek, offered her labor and equipment without any charge. We even had the visas cleared in advance this time—all we needed to do was buy the plane tickets.

DEPARTMENT OF THE ARMY

BATTALION SURGEON

1ˢᵗ BATTALION, 502D INFANTRY REGIMENT

101ˢᵀ AIRBORNE DIVISION (AIR ASSAULT)

FOB JUSTICE

APO, AE 09378

REPLY TO

ATTENTION OF:

AFZB-KB-G-SN   22 July 2008

MEMORANDUM FOR RECORD

SUBJECT: Hope.MD Nonprofit Foundation Request for CERP Funding

1. **SITUATION:**

b. The National Iraqi Assistance Center (NIAC) is the sole organization within the Ministry of Health (MOH) that provides specialized medical care and surgical interventions for children. It appears to be staffed by a single physician of unknown medical training.

c. Soldiers in the 1-502nd Infantry have established the legal infrastructure for a 501(c)3 nonprofit foundation to build a bridge between the NIAC and university medical centers that have volunteered to help children in need of surgery.

d. The Foundation, called Hope.MD, built the website www.hope.md after consulting with previous professional contacts at the Mass General Hospital laboratory of computer science.

e. Hope.MD successfully sponsored and evacuated a child for reconstructive burn surgery at the University of Cincinnati Shriner's Hospital. This surgery saved the child's limbs.

f.   Both Dartmouth College and Johns Hopkins University have agreed to sponsor additional children for surgery. Specifically, an eye surgeon at Johns Hopkins will be traveling to Turkey on August 20th to perform corneal transplantations on ten children for free.

g.   The ten children have visas and passports arranged.

h.   There is a shortage of funding for the airplane tickets and other expenses associated with the trip.

2.   CHRONOLOGY OF DEVELOPMENTS:

a.   OCT 2007: The 1-502nd Infantry is deployed in theater.

b.   NOV 2007: The Hope.MD concept is vetted and discussed among MAJ Bhavsar, CPT John Knight, CPT Jon Heavey, and their IA counterparts.

c.   DEC 2007: An initial website is built, and attorneys at Sidley & Austin LLP establish the Hope.MD Corporation with an autonomous EIN.

d.   JAN 2008: Attempts to evacuate a child for heart surgery are unsuccessful. The child dies during the delay in processing.

e.   FEB 2008: JAG provides authorization for Hope.MD to participate as an external entity to recruit funding for additional children.

f.   MAR 2008: A formal 501(c)3 tax-exempt nonprofit foundation application is filed with the IRS.

g.   APR 2008: A child is successfully evacuated via the NIAC to the University of Cincinnati Shriner's Hospital. In the course of coordination, contacts are made with the ICMI, an international NGO sponsored by retired General ********.

h.   MAY 2008: The President of Dartmouth College, James Wright, agrees to accept a child for free reconstructive burn surgery.

i.   MAY 2008: ICMI locates a surgeon from Johns Hopkins who will fly to Turkey to perform corneal transplants. Ten children are enrolled and screened for surgery.

j.   JUL 2008: Funding for the eye transplantation trip from the Iraqi MOH budget is short approximately $7k. Hope.MD remains within the IRS mandatory 501(c)3 grace period and therefore has not been able to make larger external requests for support.

3.   FUNDING REQUEST:

k.   According to the ICMI, they are in need of $7,000 for immediate disbursement to purchase plane tickets for the ten children and their guardians. Flight discounts are being arranged through United Airlines corporate headquarters, and initial talks indicate future flights may be significantly less expensive.

4.   FUTURE PLANNING:

a.   Conceptually the Hope.MD Foundation is built to create "patients without borders" whereby University medical centers extend their considerable resources and goodwill to help alleviate the humanitarian crisis.

b. Online sponsors have the ability to 'virtually adopt' any child to sponsor for surgery in a unique social networking application. This application enables sponsors to exchange pictures and messages with the children while they are in the hospital, and also enables sponsors to meet other participants in their communities.

c. Ultimately, if the MOH and other state level resources so desire, medical professionals in training could accompany the children during their trips to learn from the advanced tertiary care and surgical techniques.

d. Cooperation with other NGOs and international organizations will help build recognition for participating universities and faculty members.

e. *The 101st 2BCT stands to gain considerable goodwill not only with the local patient population, but also with the Iraqi medical community and participating universities.*

5. POC for this memorandum is the undersigned @ VOIP 6**-***8, or jonathan.heavey@******.mil

Jonathan Heavey, M.D.

CPT, MC, Battalion Surgeon

I dialed up the satellite again and submitted the CERP application to my chain of command. Thankfully the satellite was still working somehow despite sandstorms that were blowing back in at the time. Operationally, I was still in Shulla about a mile down from what we called "Shit Creek." The name wasn't particularly creative, of course, but it was definitely appropriate. The combination of the smell in the air and grit in my mouth was, as we liked to say, "magically delicious." I knew I wouldn't hear about CERP funding for some time, but I was hoping that despite our surroundings, we had finally found a way to tap into institutional resources to help the project grow. If we could find even minimal CERP support, we could help ten children regain their vision in one fell swoop. I sat there in the squalor hoping that someone somewhere in the chain of command would be as excited as we were to try to make it happen.

CHAPTER 12
$2,500 TO TAKE A SHIT

I received orders a few days later to roll back out to the Kadamiyah hospital to check on a critically wounded Iraqi police officer. I tried to explain to my infantry commander that under the MEDROE I would not be authorized to transport the man out of the Kadamiyah hospital, but the order had come from above so I did the best I could to execute what I was told.

I always hated functioning in sandstorms brownouts without surveillance or air coverage over our heads. JAM fighters would take advantage of the situation by putting out roadside bombs and picking off convoy patrols with snipers. It was my little girl's second birthday back home, and all I kept thinking as we rolled out on the mission was that I didn't want to die on my daughter's birthday. Since we already knew Kadamiyah was a dirty JAM hotspot, it was obvious to me that the wounded officer lying in the "hospital" was either a part of JAM himself, or he would soon be killed by them anyway. All we were doing was some bullshit mission that someone in the Green Zone had dreamed up to try to score points with the local sheiks. We liked to call it "kissing cheeks with sheiks," and it usually cost us men whenever someone in the rear came up with brilliant ideas like this.

As we were planning the mission, we went through the medevac scenarios we planned for if we got hit or ambushed. Our men laid out the usual orders: if we were hit by an IED, we would have to wait for a QRF (quick response force) to drive out to the scene to protect any damaged equipment before we initiated casualty evacuations. There is nothing quite as sobering as knowing full well that your four-hundred-thousand-dollar life insurance policy is a much cheaper bill for your government to pay than the fifteen million dollars it has to prioritize by protecting the equipment. Somebody got blown up? Quick! Protect the electronics in the Humvee!

Having been to Kadamiyah before, I knew what to expect, and I was not disappointed this time around, either. The JAM guards greeted us with the same knowing looks, undoubtedly fantasizing about shooting us in the back on our way out of the building. Our platoon had to move tactically again, creating the odd but necessary scenario where infantrymen cordon off one hospital hallway after another. Families anywhere nearby quickly grabbed their children and moved away from us as fast as possible. The same excited chatter broke out on the radios, and this time I could actually make out the word "Ameriki!" (Americans) being shouted.

I greatly admired our company commander, and I have no doubt he is capable of being the chairman of the Joint Chiefs of Staff someday. I would go through hell and back for him, and I consider him to be a great personal friend. But unfortunately he was tactically brilliant and completely insensitive to the diplomatic cluster fuck we were creating yet again, just like the last time. He marched into the hospital shouting out the name of the wounded officer we were looking for loudly enough for everyone to hear. We had no other way of knowing how or where to find the patient. After shouting the name out enough times to enough people, we found our way to the right ward. By the time we got there, Helen Keller would have known that our bull had arrived in the china shop.

When we approached his bedside, the officer looked at me—clearly still hurting from extensive battle injuries—and the desperate look in his eyes said it all. He had already been sneaky enough to convince the JAM guards that he was on their side, so he had managed to survive somehow (probably, as a matter of fact, because he was in JAM). Now, we were marking him in the clearest way possible as a primary assassination target since it was evident he had cooperated with the Americans in some way.

I had nothing to offer the guy from a medical standpoint. He already had an external intestinal collection bag from a rather advanced surgical procedure that someone had managed to perform on him. One of the physicians from the ward came out to see what was happening, and it was apparent that he was no fool. He didn't say hello; he just started to ask me questions in well-practiced English.

"Why do you want this man?"

"I can't speak to that."

"Who did he kill?"

"I am just a doctor."

"Is he a terrorist or an intelligence agent?"

"No."

I was trying to tap-dance my way out of the situation as quickly as possible. I turned my attention back to the patient's medical chart, trying to be polite to the physician. I knew it was too late, though. The physicians at Kadamiyah relied on JAM for protection. We had marked this man with a giant bull's eye. Even if the hole in his intestines healed, I was sure he was going to get torture holes drilled into his skull before he was executed.

A short time later, our unit caught a Caucasian Irishman from the Irish Republican Army (IRA) who was holed up with some JAM bomb makers in Kadamiyah as well. I was asked to treat him and "patch him up," although nobody would say what his wounds were before they brought him to me. I deferred to higher levels at the combat support hospital, as I got the distinct sense it was an issue that went well over my pay grade. None of us knew why or how a white, English-speaking Irishman would be hanging out with JAM bomb makers in our sector. MI-6, the British intelligence agency, had long ago infiltrated the IRA at the most senior levels, so I had my own conspiracy theories about the guy. The only way to get inside JAM was to offer them some "chicken feed," or agents who appeared to be sympathetic to their cause by helping them build and plant bombs. To this day I wonder if the wounded police officer in the Kadamiyah hospital was related to the IRA agent who was later arrested by our forces. I have to believe the IRA agent got the better half of that deal, as we rarely used drill bits to extract information from our sources.

After visiting Kadamiyah, we were all relieved to be off the roads and back at the warehouse in Shulla. Thankfully nobody had been hit in our convoy, though the sandstorm continued to rage on. With the magically delicious taste in our mouths, we decided against talking about endless nachos and turned instead to an improvised game of Pictionary to pass the time.

It was the perfect antidote to the intensity of the mission and the day. Nobody knew it at the time, but it turned out that our very own Sergeant Parker was the world's greatest Pictionary player. Even though he can't draw for shit himself, he could instantly guess whatever anyone on his team was drawing. At one point someone drew a stick figure with what looked something like a gun in his hand. Parker, using his secret Jedi Pictionary powers, knew in two seconds that the stick figure was the Terminator. Apparently they play a lot of Pictionary in the swamplands of Louisiana. I guess it beats sticking a fishing pole in an alligator's mouth.

* * *

As time passed and the weeks went by, I didn't hear back about my application for CERP funding. I went through the usual process following up with anyone I could find in the chain of command to try to figure out who could authorize the decision. While my immediate medical supervisor was a great guy who was always incredibly supportive, he didn't have CERP budgetary authority since that went through a non-medical chain of command. I was pushing uphill again, asking superiors from too many levels above me in a separate chain of authority about something that wasn't in their lane. In the counter insurgency manual CERP funding was described as the easiest to use "rapid response" funds that battalion-level commanders could use at their discretion, but my application had apparently gone into no-man's bureaucracy land and nobody in our sector had CERP money to work with.

As the cut-off date approached for the ten children to receive eye surgeries, John and I decided to just put in whatever funds we could from ourselves and our family friends. I wrote a quick journal entry later that day, as I had grown weary of all the excuses and roadblocks we had encountered in our efforts:

The Value of Vision

> *"Sir, if you can allocate $7k from the $52 million dollar CERP budget, I can send ten children to Johns Hopkins to have their corneas repaired and their vision restored."*
>
> *Seven hundred dollars a child, all costs included, to transform them from blind and crippled to fully capable of accomplishing anything they want in their lives.*
>
> *Shockingly, the chain of command never replied with authorization. Seven thousand is no small sum. But relative to the $4.3 million that was just spent trying to fix a pool for the Iraqi Army ass-clowns to swim in, it is nothing.*
>
> *And yet, it is everything.*

By the time I left Shulla to return to the dungeon, John and I were heading back toward square one again. We were fed up with the lack of help from the PRT, USAID, CERP, and other federal programs. Every headline we saw in Western media was about hearts and minds, while the reality we saw on the ground was the same brutal mess day in and day out. Even though we had managed to finally get one starfish back in the ocean, we couldn't find a way to build on what we had done.

We were lifting weights one day when we found the perfect outlet for what seemed like our never-ending frustration. We were curling dumbbells—grunting, sweating, and pissed off at every dirty stinking piece of crap that surrounded us. And then it hit us—*contractors*. Defense and oil industry contractors were *everywhere* in Iraq. If the State Department Provincial Reconstruction Teams didn't have funds, and USAID didn't have funds, and CERP didn't have funds, and the Red Cross didn't have funds, and the NGO foundations didn't have funds...well, hell, *we knew exactly who DID have funds*. The biggest defense and oil industry contractors had to be making at least some money off of all this, so why not ask them to pitch in and match the money we had come up with? It's not like they would miss a couple thousand dollars.

Excited by the idea, I set the satellite connection for continuous download once again. Every ten to twelve hours it would download an annual report from the top defense and oil industry companies. Over the course of two weeks, I compiled the security and exchange commission (SEC) reports for the largest contractors in the war. I set up my caffeine shrine once again, and sat down to read each report from front to back. I went through each one extremely carefully, struggling to understand the complex corporate analysis reports. As I read through their statements on corporate responsibility, I compared them with the contents of the counterinsurgency manual. It was fascinating stuff, and tedious beyond belief. Thankfully, the need to perpetually swat at horseflies kept me alert enough to prevent my eyes from completely glazing over.

Page after page, I thumbed through revenue metrics and complex balance sheet data. Each report was full of colorful pictures of employees high on Prozac, smiling gleefully alongside their bosses. Of course, every CEO was smiling broadly, too, happily offering inspiring quotes about their benevolent influence on the world and the love they were so diligently working to spread to humanity.

I searched specifically for SEC forms 10-K and DEF 14-A, two obscure filings that every publicly traded company is required to report every year. The 10-K data had detailed information on the company-wide earnings and equity structure, while the DEF 14-A spelled out specifically how the corporate leadership was paid. Let me say that again: the DEF 14-A is a public listing that quantifies exactly how much each of these incredibly powerful CEOs earns each year.

I expected that I would find some increase in income as a result of the war, as it would only make sense to me. As a self-respecting capitalist, I wouldn't actually have it any other way. These companies build massive security mechanisms that protect all of us in ways most of us will never fully appreciate. They bring a tremendous amount of value to our society and to our world by helping us to maintain stability and security. Like the fictional Tony Stark character says in the *Ironman* movies: "It's the American way, and it's worked pretty well for us so far."

But none of that prepared me to see the data that I saw. The increases in profits for these companies were unbelievable in size and scope. The information and data were utterly mind-boggling to me. Company after company had boosted its top line revenue by an insane amount in just one year-to-year comparison. What's more, their bottom line costs didn't change all that significantly, so their profit margins had grown exponentially from the war. The CEO and board of director compensation metrics increased exponentially as well, both in terms of cash income and equity payments from the growth of the company. They were clearing out two decades' worth of inventory at a markup, and pocketing every penny in the process.

My favorite example was United Technologies, a company I had never even heard of before I looked in the SEC records. The company boosted its revenues by $11,000,000,000 (eleven billion) dollars in just one year-to-year comparison of prewar and wartime SEC filings. What's more, the CEO himself increased his personal earnings from $4,200,000 (over four million) dollars during peacetime to an astounding $38,000,000 (thirty-eight million) in *one year of war*. That's a 904.7% increase in personal income! If a worker earning $50,000 experienced the same markup, they would earn $452,380 in one year! I did some simple math, and working on the assumption the CEO worked about fifty hours a week for fifty weeks a year, he earned roughly $5 a second, $250 a minute, and $15,200 an hour! I was so stunned I had to find John and tell him about the numbers.

"Do you realize that if this motherfucker bends over to pick up a five-dollar bill, it's a waste of his time?" John was his usual nonchalant self in his reply: "Makes me wonder how much he'd get to take a shit." Assuming a ten-minute potty break, the answer was $2,500! Two thousand five hundred dollars to take a shit!

Now, I'm sure that a CEO probably has to work much more than fifty hours a week, so if you double that figure to a hundred hours a week, the poor guy would only make $7,600 an hour, or $1,250 dollars a crap. Still, the point was pretty clear. We were on a never-ending mission in the middle of a shithole, and a bunch of really rich elitists were using our patriotism to subsidize their profit margins.

I decided I would fire up a letter to ask these fine leaders for some help, and to challenge them to match the funds we had already raised for the foundation. In the letter, I compiled their income data into a chart and juxtaposed it with photographs from the carnage we had witnessed on the ground. I added in my favorite inspiring quotes from their annual reports to help highlight the essential elements of their corporate social responsibility policies. Here is a sampling of what the challenge letter looked like:

Dear *******,

Greetings from sunny Kadamiyah, Baghdad! Over the past year we have been working to set up a 501(c)3 nonprofit foundation here in Iraq. As you may know, large organizations such as the UN, Red Cross, Doctors Without Borders, and Unicef have been forced to flee the violence here. We built this foundation to help the humanitarian crisis we see every day. As far as we can tell, there are no other options.

We would like to offer you a friendly challenge. Using our own funding, we have helped nearly a dozen children receive surgery for life-threatening and disabling conditions. According to the revenue and income metrics below, it appears to us that you have considerably greater resources to help more children. **We would like to challenge you to match, dollar for dollar, any contributions we are able to raise from the internet community.**

We have juxtaposed the quotes of your corporate responsibility statements in your annual reports with pictures of what we are experiencing here on the ground. This is not intended to appear sensational or to imply culpability; it is simply meant to draw attention to a crisis that has gone unreported and unrepaired for far too long.

We realize you have a massive fiduciary responsibility to a wide range of constituents, and we genuinely intend to fairly portray the complexity of the challenges you face in your management decisions. That being said, we hope you will help us live up to the ethical standards you embrace and accept this challenge. We take you at your word when you speak of ideals designed to improve the human condition. However, we recall being told that all it takes for evil to flourish is for good men to do nothing. Which begs the question: what will you do?

Sincerely,

Jon Heavey, M.D.
John Knight, P.A.

Pre-war v. current financial data, per SEC Form 10-K and DEF-14A annual reports

Defense Contractors (top ten by US DOD payables)	Revenue ($ millions)			Post-Tax Net Income ($ millions)			CEO Compensation ($ millions)		
	2002	2007	Increase	2002	2007	Increase	2002	2007	Increase
Lockheed Martin	26,578	41,862	15,284	500	3,033	2,533	11.7	18.6	6.9
Boeing	53,831	66,387	12,556	492	4,074	3,582	3.9	19.0	15.1
Northrop Grumman	17,206	32,018	14,812	64	1,790	1,726	9.4	20.6	11.2
General Dynamics	13,829	27,240	13,411	917	2,072	1,155	7.9	18.6	10.7
Raytheon	16,760	21,301	4,541	(640)	2,578	3,218	3.7	19.3	15.6
Halliburton	12,572	22,576	10,004	(998)	2,348	3,346	7.8	17.0	9.2
United Technologies	28,212	39,240	11,028	2,236	4,224	1,988	4.2	38.0	33.8
Science Applications Intl	6,095	8,061	1,966	19	391	372	2	6.9	4.9
Computer Science Corp	11,426	14,857	3,431	344	388	44	1.7	17.0	15.3
Humana Inc	422	25,290	24,868	142	834	692	1.7	10.3	8.6
	Total Increase:		$111,901 million	Total Increase:		$18,656 million	Total Increase:		$131 million

Oil Contractors (four primary MOI firms[1])	Revenue($ millions)			Post-Tax Net Income ($ millions)			CEO Compensation ($ millions)		
	2002	2007	Increase	2002	2007	Increase	2002	2007	Increase
Exxon-Mobil	204,500	390,328	185,828	11,500	40,610	29,110	5.5	16.7	11.2
Shell ([2]Netherlands)	*222,768	355,782	133,014	*9,656	31,926	22,270	*3.4	9.0	5.6
Total Inc ([2]*France)	150,734	233,365	82,631	8,752	19,896	11,144	3.5	'4.1	0.6
British Petroleum- BP ([2]England)	*178,721	284,365	105,644	*8,395	21,169	12,774	'4.5	'4.1	(0.4)
	Total Increase:		$507,117 million	Total Increase:		$75,298 million	Total Increase:		$17 million

1 Press Release, 19 June 2008, NY Times/IHT, http://www.iht.com/articles/2008/06/19/africa/19iraq.php

2 Data compiled via Form 20-F (international) in lieu of SEC 10-K & DEF-14A

* Publicly reported data after significant merger and acquistion activity; may include currency conversions, pro-forma calculations, or re-stated earnings. Data subject to standard variances between EU & US GAAP

' CEO compensation data limited to base salary due to change in management, variances in lumped equity distributions (EDIP), and long term incentive payments (LTIP).

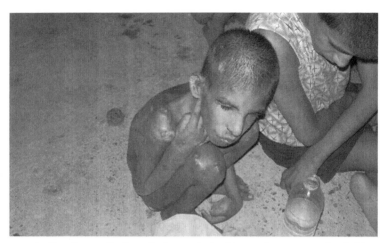

At Raytheon, all of our business relationships with customers, shareholders, employees, suppliers, and host communities must rest on a foundation of integrity and trust. Our success is dependent on each individual's commitment to these enduring values, and no success is worth the expense of compromising ethical behavior.

Halliburton people commit thousands of hours to community outreach projects—supporting schools, cleaning beaches and deserts, planting trees—because that's what it means to be a good neighbor.

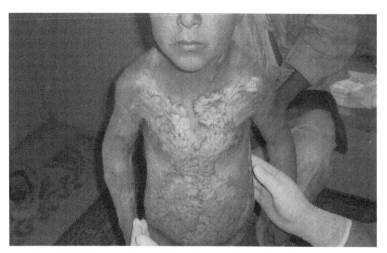

ExxonMobil is an active participant in every community where we operate. We make community investments to support programs in our key focus areas of health, education and biodiversity.

* * *

I was told by numerous people over the years that the series of photographs we chose were too disturbing, and that it was disrespectful to put them next to the pull quotes on corporate social responsibility. The photos are incredibly disturbing, and tragically that is exactly the point. People don't see these pictures in civilian life, and they don't face the gruesome ground level realities of war. I would think any leader who saw pictures like this would want to intervene immediately to help alleviate such atrocious suffering. As I said in the letter, it is not my intent to blame these CEOs, as they carry a massive fiduciary responsibility to their shareholders that few of us can fathom. But they are leaders, and they are capable of acting on information that is brought to them, just like you and I are capable of acting on problems that are brought to our attention.

When I put the letter together, I assumed there would be significant fallout from my request to these companies. Even though the CEOs were civilians who had no relationship to my chain of command, only a fool would think they didn't share a very close relationship with the senior-most levels of the authority structure. I wanted to be very careful by prefacing the letter to indicate why we had issued such a challenge, and I attempted to mitigate the disturbing nature of the challenge by sending each leader a handwritten note to explain what we were seeing outside the wire in combat.

I also went through formal JAG consultation channels to be certain that what I was doing was compliant with all UCMJ (uniform code of military justice) and federal statutes. The junior JAG officers who saw what I did were excited, off the record, of course, that John and I were challenging the contractors. Like us, they had seen enough to wonder how anyone could be profiting so much from the war. They advised me, though, that I had to add various disclaimers to clarify that the foundation was not related to the DoD and was an autonomous 501(c)3.

The JAG officers also told me I had to remove the word "soldier" in my letter since this implied a relationship to the military. I found that to be another entertaining wrinkle in the legal wrangling, but I complied with their recommendations. John and I had only just recently been able to prove we weren't terrorists, and we now apparently had to clarify that we also weren't soldiers. I thought maybe we could just call ourselves "American dudes wandering around Iraq who happen to wear body armor, carry weapons, and treat really sick kids," but I figured the letter was probably already contentious enough of an approach as it was.

I postmarked all the envelopes with my usual APO AE address and sent them out via the "combat mail" free postage. We didn't really expect to get any response, but it was cathartic to send them nonetheless. The mail typically took a month or two to get back to the States, so we just waited to see what would happen.

Around this time, my boss's boss, a division surgeon who was from a different unit that I didn't have any relationship with, started to hear that I was working on this initiative. He contacted me to inform me that someone at criminal investigation division (CID) had threatened to open an inquiry on me and other men in my unit on unrelated charges. CID is an extremely serious matter with huge professional implications—in effect, it was a threat that criminal charges could be initiated and I would never be able to practice medicine again (or much, much worse). To this day I find his timing on the matter to be rather suspect.

The pretense that was given for the CID inquiry involved medicines that our unit had given away to the Iraqi Army. We had been donating our expiring medications to our Iraqi Army counterpart, Colonel M, for several months. He had nothing to treat his patients with so he was happy to use our expiring medications rather than throw them in the trash. Expiring medicines routinely get thrown away years before they need to be thrown away, largely because it helps ensure the company that sells the medicine will have continuously renewing orders. From a safety standpoint, there was no concern whatsoever. I would have given the antibiotics to my own child, even if the label had a "sell by" date that was going to run out in a few months. Colonel M accepted this as well and documented that he accepted responsibility on his medical license if he chose to use the medications after the formal expiration date.

We also fully documented the donation on our end to be certain we were complying with all statutes and regulations. A portion of the medicines we donated were morphine injectors, and due to the sensitive nature of narcotic controls, we made certain we documented, photographed, and inventoried the morphine injectors with independently corroborated witnesses. The fact we were so careful about the whole thing is probably what caused somebody in CID to wonder what the heck was going on in the first place.

Thankfully, Colonel M hadn't even touched the morphine injectors and we were able to take them back from him. We then photographed the entire medical inventory again and had three witnesses document their destruction. It was yet another moment of sheer brilliance—taking away effective medicine from our supposed ally to throw it in the trash bin before his eyes.

CID promptly dropped the inquiry when they realized that they were wasting everybody's time with a pointless witch-hunt. But that didn't stop the division surgeon from passing along his words of wisdom very clearly to me. It was obvious he was not happy that we had taken some initiative of our own to solve a problem, rather than sitting around doing nothing and throwing away the medicine. He didn't hide his annoyance with me, and I still remember his words of admonishment. He told me, with a straight face, "Jon, just because you can do something doesn't mean you should. You have to do what is right." In his twisted mind, it was "right" to throw away medicine rather than donate it to people who desperately needed it. Remind me again, good sir, how does that sit with the Hippocratic oath? Which part of the counterinsurgency manual says that is the right thing to do? Which part of the Bible, Koran, or Torah says that is right? Now that you threatened me, unsuccessfully, with a bullshit criminal inquiry that went nowhere, what other pleasantries do you have in mind?

The division surgeon had known at many different points that we had put a lot of effort into evacuating the kids for surgery, and, quite frankly, I think he was envious of the fact his subordinates had found a workaround for a problem that plagued his sector. I wrote to my dad over e-mail to tell him about what had transpired and to ask him if he had ever experienced similar scenarios during his time in Vietnam. My dad was a career naval officer and his reply was priceless: "Sounds like you had a great day with a REMF'r, my son. That's Rear-Echelon-Mother-Fucker. Just remember, dance pretty in your dress whites, keep your head down, and let him have his moment. When he leaves, he'll still be an REMF'r and you will still be a leader."

Thanks, Dad. I love you.

CHAPTER 14
PANCAKE MAN

"No, it's not called an ice machine; it's called a Zamboni."

"Surh, uh, it ain't my spot to say nuthin' but y'aunt ti learn you sumthin usefah tuhday?"

"Sure, Carr, you're right. I'm all ears, what do you got?"

"I ain't nevah used no fancy French wurd like that fir no Yankee ice machine, but I been fraw geggin wit moonshine and ben kickt outta Waffle House. So lemme teacha whachu need ta know when you git yur nose outta dem der books."

Specialist Carr was my favorite medic. He got me spun up and learned real good. By the time I was in the thick of the deployment, I knew the lyrics to any Lynyrd Skynyrd song you could name, the current rankings for every college football team in the SEC, and how to say "fraw geggin" instead of "frog gigging." In my Yankee naïveté, I had never even learned how much fun it can be to drink moonshine and spear frogs with a giant fork in infested swamps. Apparently the War of Northern Aggression ain't over yet.

Despite the education and learning Carr passed on to me, the days back at the dungeon started to blend together as the deployment carried on. The pattern became routine: sick call in the morning, exercise when we could, heat casualties in the afternoon, and mortars/casualties shortly after dinner. Sprinkle in the occasional IED blast or small arms fire on roads nearby, and you pretty much get the picture.

John and I kept pressing forward to evacuate more kids as best as we could, though we had basically exhausted our means to continue funding the effort. Rafal, the child we had evacuated for burn surgery, had been having a surprising amount of difficulty in Cincinnati. He was not old enough to function independently or care for his surgical wounds, and, due to cultural barriers, his grandmother could not effectively discipline him to prevent him from infecting his wounds. He was a little boy who thought he was a man. He resented the surgeons for helping him, as he only knew the pain from what he was going through.

An old friend of mine from high school, Ellen Maxwell, had worked really hard to set up a local television report about Rafal that I had hoped would help open the door for more cases behind him. She had coordinated with reporters in other states and producers at various stations to arrange everything related to the story. The day the news crews traveled to the house in Cincinnati where Rafal was staying, his grandmother reneged on her prior commitments and decided instead that she wouldn't let them film anything related to his case. She was too afraid to have even his feet or pixelated image shown on TV, for fear of being killed in retribution when they returned. It was devastating, as our whole project depended on people hearing about the cases to build momentum for other children. While I certainly understood her hesitation, the inability to even show his feet kicking a soccer ball was so restrictive it made it impossible for the news crews to do a story. Ellen, who had gone to so much trouble on our behalf, ended up wasting considerable time and resources when the news crews got turned away at the last minute.

I have to admit the whole escapade was really upsetting. We had gone to such extensive lengths to provide care for Rafal, yet his grandmother couldn't even convince him to keep his wounds clean. We had been highly sensitive to his safety and privacy concerns and we had asked her extensively about them in advance. We would never have even considered a story in the news without her blessing, yet she waited until other people had wasted precious resources and time. She had sabotaged the effort for dozens of kids who could have come after her own grandson.

To make matters worse, one day with no warning, she decided she wanted to leave America and return to Iraq. Her grandson's treatments weren't even complete yet. When people tried to convince her to stay, she began to have bizarre medical complaints and symptoms. The family who she stayed with was concerned for her so they took her to the emergency room on multiple occasions, paying out of pocket for extensive testing and precautionary measures. Nothing turned up, and she and her grandson left the country before his surgeries and rehabilitation were complete. It was not exactly the way a feel-good story was supposed to unfold. At the rate things were going with our first starfish, it would be impossible to build momentum for other children to get surgery. After the glimmer of hope that came with our first successful evacuation, it was pretty devastating to see what transpired.

Sometime after we heard the news about Rafal, John and I came across an unusual sight while we were wandering the halls of FOB Justice. We saw a guy who appeared to be a Westerner who wasn't wearing body armor, and he looked like he might be a reporter. The sight of a reporter outside the Green Zone unaccompanied by a platoon of media affairs personnel was completely unique to us. We decided we should take a chance and talk with him to see if he might be able to help us out with the project we had been working on. We had been warned on numerous occasions that any discussions with members of the media were to be handled by media affairs personnel only, but by this point in the deployment, we just didn't really care anymore.

The reporter, Ernesto Londono, turned out to be a truly rare professional. He had found ways to travel independently of his own accord, which seemed incredibly dangerous to both of us. We could only imagine what the bounty on his head would be if he got kidnapped. To this day I think he had to be insane to do his job given the risks involved. Yet there he was—a congenial and soft-spoken guy who happened to travel around Iraq like a bulletproof superhero.

Ernesto cashed in all kinds of chips with his superiors to help us out with the foundation project. He made several trips around Baghdad in a regular car, passing through checkpoints and risking his life to help cover the story. I remember meeting up with him again at the gate to our base one day—more specifically, I remember how tricky it was to figure out how to describe where to meet. The phones didn't work, as usual, and I didn't know what kind of directions to give him. "Um, turn left at the place where the IED blew up yesterday, and then turn right where the snipers like to hang out. When you come up to a creek that smells like shit, you're getting close. When you come to a road that nobody other than our infantrymen call 'Cubs North,' turn right! Just ask a local how to say 'Cubs North' in Arabic, and I'm sure they'll point you in the right direction!"

Ernesto went to great lengths to cover the foundation in the *Washington Post*, which was a huge breakthrough. Despite the risks to his career, he included our challenge to the defense and oil industry leaders in his piece. The article talked about the hurdles we had overcome in the process, including the fact we had to prove to our own government that we weren't terrorists. It was a great day when the story ran, as almost immediately we started to receive a flood of donations and offers for help. We thought that maybe the other children we had identified could still get help after all.

Not surprisingly, shortly after the story ran, we also received word from higher-ups that we had "raised red flags" and were walking on thin ice. I got messages from senior JAG lawyers who told me I had violated regulations when I was photographed "in uniform" for the article. I had thought that might be brought up at some point, so I had specifically removed my uniform shirt and nameplate at the time. I was only in a brown T-shirt when the picture was taken. Hey, I didn't say I was a soldier. I'm just an American guy in Iraq who happens to wear a brown undershirt that matches what everyone wears underneath their uniform.

Unfortunately, the threats from senior-level lawyers didn't stop there. They told me I had potentially violated the law by "soliciting on behalf of a non-military organization" even though the article contained no solicitation whatsoever. They sent John intimidating messages telling him he had violated e-mail policies when he sent messages to his friends asking for help. Some of his friends, shockingly, happened to have Army e-mail addresses, and apparently the lawyers felt it was illegal for his message to go to someone with an Army e-mail account. Our efforts to go through the WeSupportYou.mil charitable networks were rejected on the same basis, and we were advised not to even try being listed on the combined federal campaign charity registry.

The senior JAG lawyers then turned to our challenge to the defense and oil leaders and started to find ways to sanction and obstruct what we had done. They made it clear that any future communications had to be controlled by the media affairs office, and they made it clear that we could face UCMJ citations for unethical behavior if we continued to press forward with our challenge.

Our time in Iraq was already more than halfway over, but our fight to build the foundation was only starting to build momentum. We weren't about to give up. Soldiers and medics from other units started to contact us and help us identify new cases after they heard what we were doing. Junior enlisted guys everywhere started to e-mail us and ask if we could help them with families they knew in their sector. Although we still didn't have major resources to work with, we politely found ways to circumvent the lawyers, and kept building the foundation.

* * *

A few weeks after the *Post* article was published, I was traveling toward the Green Zone again on an in-theater "rest and relaxation" program. It is designed to take a soldier's mind off combat for a bit, which is a useful and benevolent intent. All I remember thinking at the time, though, was that it meant another road trip through Injun country. As far as I could tell from the mutilated men I had seen, it sure as hell wasn't worth a casual drive through the slums of Baghdad to go sit by a pool in the Green Zone. Thankfully, a cousin of mine back home knew a friend who was stationed at the embassy, and he apparently knew a way we could share a cold beer together. Sitting by a pool might not be worth risking your life, but finding a cold beer in the middle of a no-alcohol war zone is a different story.

The night we were getting ready to leave, one of my medics made a nonchalant comment about our convoy and the time everyone was leaving. Unfortunately he said it out loud in front of a large group of contractors who were local Iraqis, including one whom I was convinced was an informant for JAM. I could have throttled my medic for being so careless, but like most things in theater, his slipup was either no big deal or potentially deadly. I decided not to "smoke" him for being an idiot, as we already had enough drama in our lives anyway.

By the time we got our shit together for the convoy, it was nighttime and the usual industrial waste was thick in the air. The Kadamiyah shrine had spotlights that started to wander the horizon near our base, which they had never done before. It looked like they were searching for something. They would shine the lights up toward our helicopters passing overhead, and toward our base gates. In the paranoia of combat, that was all I needed to be convinced that the dirty informant on our base had told them about our convoy departure plans. Thankfully I was wrong, but as usual I had no way of knowing until we were out of range and had not been targeted by snipers in the mosque.

I arrived in the Green Zone without any significant events on the convoy, and I racked out for the night in an old republican palace that had been converted to barracks. It had toilets that flushed that also had normal plastic seats and no chemical feces soup beneath it. I remember how strange that felt the first time my ass touched a clean seat in a room that didn't stink to high heaven. Outside the building, you could see other high-rise buildings, many of which had holes in the walls from mortar rounds and other explosives. It was like a contemporary painting—nouveau riche with authentic combat austerity blown into select parts. I felt like a yuppie tourist on a camping trip in a war zone.

It turns out the place we were staying in was called "FOB Freedom," which was a little ironic. It had a really nice hotel-type building, swimming pools, and other luxuries that stood in stark contrast to everything else in the country. There was only one catch—you couldn't leave FOB Freedom. It was on lockdown. It was inside the Green Zone, but they didn't want soldiers to escape and run to the combat support hospital looking for a medical evacuation. As a result, FOB Freedom had a perimeter that was guarded and locked, like most prison complexes in America.

I exchanged some e-mails with my cousin's friend at the embassy, who apparently knew how to find a beer somewhere in the Green Zone. It was difficult to check e-mail or respond in a timely way so I figured there wouldn't be much chance it could actually work out. I had almost forgotten about it when one day a junior NCO came running up to me by the pool. He was out of breath and clearly had important matters on his mind. "Captain Heavey, sir, there is a State Department official here with embassy credentials who has issued an order for you to be transferred under his custody." My heart skipped a beat with excitement. Normally I would cringe when I heard the word "orders" or "under custody" but this time I had a fleeting hope: this might, just might, be the key to finding a cold beer.

I followed the NCO into the building and was introduced to Mike S[6], an unassuming but thoroughly impressive gentleman who also happened to be the longest-tenured state department

---

[6] Name modified for privacy

representative in Iraq. I didn't know it at the time but Mike had already *lived* in Iraq for *four years.* As a physician, I will say that is grounds to certify insanity, as nobody in their right mind would ever spend that kind of time in that shithole. Mike was a former airborne grunt who had figured out how to make the levers of logistics work in the Green Zone long ago. With his chrome Suburban and State Department ID, Mike had every official at FOB Freedom convinced that he was authorized to arrest me for questioning and escort me off FOB Freedom for interrogation. I have never been so utterly thrilled to be arrested in my life.

After a half-hour delay processing paperwork, I strolled out to Mike's SUV without my weapon. My weapon had been turned in previously with the paperwork processing, and as strange as it may sound, I felt completely naked without it. I had to keep telling myself that I was OK inside the Green Zone and that we were with Americans. But Mike and his friends didn't have weapons on them, either, and it was distinctly uncomfortable to be off FOB Freedom without a weapon and ammunition at my side.

Mike was kind enough to take me by the main headquarters for US operations inside Saddam's republican palace. Cameras were not allowed inside, so unfortunately I couldn't take a photograph. It was completely surreal to be in his headquarters. It looked like any other office, but with oddly dysfunctional amenities. There was a cafeteria with open seating where everyone was socializing like in a regular office building. Yet, in the same area there were hundreds of plywood cubicles constructed, and everywhere you looked there were loose wires and printer cables running along the ground. It was like a scene out of Dilbert, crossed with Bob Villa's home improvement.

Overhead, Saddam had commissioned ornate paintings—including a giant portrait of himself carrying a rifle. He also had an entire wall full of Scud missiles firing off toward an Israeli flag. On the far side of the space I could see a water cooler with a small group gathered around it. I wondered what gossip they were sharing under the watchful presence of Saddam's oversized mustache mural.

Mike knew everybody in the headquarters, and my head was spinning as he introduced me to his colleagues. Everyone there had these incredibly impressive backgrounds. Many were from top-flight schools and universities. I lost track of how many PhDs and JDs were busily running around, sipping a latte from the cafeteria while also sporting desert boots. It was like this land of make-believe—as if the entire faculty of my old university had teleported across the globe into a war zone and acquired funny looking boots on the way. I was wondering why nobody had a chalkboard handy so we could take in some lessons on differential equations, inorganic chemistry, or the emerging fashion of Mesopotamia.

Eventually we wrapped up at the headquarters and Mike took the SUV back out to a local store in the Green Zone. As we bounced along the pockmarked dirt roads, he pointed out the location for a completely Westernized convenience store. It was tucked quietly and unobtrusively behind a group of buildings. He walked inside, and since I was still in uniform, I stood by waiting for him to buy some "spirits" for the evening. As I stood there, I was again uncomfortable without my weapon, though the various European diplomats walking all around me were completely at ease with their surroundings. Local Iraqi merchants zipped by on their scooters at uncomfortably close distances. I instinctively was afraid they had weapons for an ambush. It was unnerving standing there "naked" without my weapon while everyone around me was laughing comfortably. The Green Zone was different in every way imaginable.

We then headed out to the new American embassy and were greeted by a ragtag team of Peruvian guards. They were hell-bent on figuring out the ID requirements and other paperwork details to determine if I could come into the embassy. As the guards fuddled through the materials, Mike and his friends just kept saying, "*Es bien*," in Spanish over and over until eventually the guards gave up. They just shook their heads, looked at me with exasperation, and agreed, "*Es bien*," as they waved me by. A note to all the terrorists in Iraq: if you really want to damage the embassy, don't waste your time lobbing mortars or faking passports. Just learn how to say, "*Es bien*."

Inside the new embassy, I was amazed to see a sparkling clean swimming pool, complete with lane markers and all the amenities you would expect at an American gym. There were also tennis courts, basketball courts, and all kinds of luxuries that reminded me of home. Mike took us up to his apartment and I was amazed to see the living quarters. It was simple by American standards but absolutely incredible by Iraqi standards. It not only had air-conditioning, there was a dishwasher and a refrigerator!

As we settled into his apartment, Mike regaled us with some of the funniest stories I had heard in a long time. He had been through so much over the years, it was incredible to hear how far he had come to be where we were sitting. He had also developed an incredibly wry sense of humor over the years, and his take on the absurdity was just hilarious.

I still remember my favorite story from that night. Mike

had been the primary state department representative during the major offensive at Fallujah. He told us that at one point a local fighter was idiotic enough to come out with an AK-47 to shoot at an oncoming convoy of M-1 Abrams tanks. The tanks were heading straight at him, and, rather predictably, the AK-47 did nothing to deter them. The fighter was shot and quickly killed, and the tanks were mid-operation so they couldn't exactly stop to remove his body from the road. As a result, dozens upon dozens of tanks ran over him one after the other.

As the story goes, the guy's mangled corpse subsequently became a focal point for operational planning. The soldiers in the units would talk to each other in tactical terms and put everything in relation to the corpse that soon became known as "pancake man." Infantry platoons would give each other directions like "go two clicks west until you get to the pancake man," or "call in indirect fire three clicks past pancake man." When I heard the legend of pancake man, it was so morbidly hilarious, I couldn't stop laughing. You know you've been in Iraq for too long when a story like that is somehow hilarious instead of deeply disturbing.

Mike and his colleagues at the State Department were quite helpful with the foundation project John and I had been working on. They understood why we had gone through all the legal hoops to form it, and they understood how their own PRT teams had been unable to participate. They had come across the challenges of stove-piped funding before, and it was a catharsis to talk with them about the efforts we had gone through to try to find help. Getting to know some friends in the Green Zone helped us immensely with passport and visa clearance challenges with the foundation in the subsequent months.

By the time the evening was over, I was feeling reinvigorated again, believing that we could make more headway with the foundation if we just kept working at it. Mike pointed me to a cab that could take me back to FOB Freedom as we parted ways. I promised him I would find a way to return the favor and get him a beer back home. Thankfully we've both been able to enjoy drinks together back on the other side of civilization since that night.

As I got into the cab, it dawned on me once again that I did not have my weapon. The driver was a local Iraqi, and if I felt uncomfortable standing outside the store before, I felt a hundred times worse in the cab. As he drove toward FOB Freedom, he had to go by a roundabout, and one of the exits off the roundabout had a direct path over a bridge that ran into Sadr City. I clenched my hand over the door handle, feeling like an idiot to be in such a dangerous position and preparing for any indication his cab was headed toward the gate by the exit. Thankfully, he was an honest contractor and he took me back to FOB Freedom. It is bizarre to think that something as inconsequential as a gate and an exit off a road can mark the difference between relaxation among friends and almost certain death. I was quite happy to report back to FOB Freedom that night, where I knew the armed guards were on my side.

* * *

By the time I got back to FOB Justice and the dungeon, Dr. Akpek from Johns Hopkins had traveled into Turkey to perform eye surgery on ten children. It was incredible to think that the whole project had come together, thanks largely to the efforts of leaders at the ICMI and other organizations. John and I had not had the opportunity to meet these children, but we wanted to contribute in any way we could. Our CERP funding had not been approved so we just donated everything we could from the collection our family and friends had pulled together. Apparently that had been enough to keep the project moving forward and for the children to receive surgery.

As the days passed, we got update reports that were encouraging. Dr. Akpek successfully restored vision for eight out of the ten children she operated on, which in the middle of the war seemed like the very definition of a miracle. She transformed their lives and the lives of their families. Eventually she and her team would forward us a picture from the airport where the group of children gathered before their operations. It is a heartwarming picture, and it was incredible to see the group of them looking like normal children outside of the vortex of war. They were able to be out of the awful mess long enough for Dr. Akpek to perform her miracle, and I hope someday somehow I can meet one of them. I would love to learn more about what they have done with their newfound vision and life.

Dr. Akpek's mission happened during a time when we were

under an increasing number of attacks from JAM. Moqtada Al-Sadr called off his ceasefire agreement and we noticed the difference almost immediately. I wrote a few journal entries around that time that help bring the ground-level realities of our world at the time back into focus:

Of Hearts and Minds

Two weeks ago I treated a militant gunman who had been shot by Iraqi Security Forces in a firefight near our base. The gunman had been shot in the right side of his chest and the bullet exited over the middle left area of his back. He couldn't breathe and appeared to be dying. The bullet had tumbled and torn through his right lung, causing it to collapse and bleed profusely. Once we opened his chest, we were able to tell his other major structures were intact. He was arguably the luckiest patient I have ever seen—the bullet managed to miss his innominate, subclavian, and aortic arteries (not to mention his heart and spine).

After we drained about a liter of blood out of his chest and re-inflated his lung, it was apparent he was going to survive. It was a satisfying case clinically, though obviously a bit bizarre to be working to save the life of someone our guards were just trying to kill. He went on to receive very sophisticated follow-up care through the best US resources available, including air medical evacuation and full trauma care for weeks afterward. Oddly enough, he was only too happy to cooperate and talk with our intelligence personnel. Something about avoiding certain death makes one oddly cooperative with the people who saved your life.

Which brings me to the strange situation I found myself in today. One of our local Iraqi workers approached me about a relative of his who was also shot during the conflicts last week, but he was a member of the Iraqi Security Forces. Unlike a considerable number of his corrupted counterparts, he actually fulfilled his duties and did not abandon his post. He was subsequently shot in the chest, too, and because of his job with the ISF was taken to the aid station on the Iraqi side of our base. He is now languishing in an Iraqi hospital where they don't have a neurosurgeon available to remove the bullet that is lodged in his posterior thorax and spine. He is dying a slow, painful death, and our local national coworker asked us if we could help by transferring him to US physicians for care.

Our MEDROE (medical rules of engagement) policy prevents me from doing so, despite many phone calls and messages asking for help. It apparently would undercut efforts from the Iraqis to bolster their own medical resources, and as a result, he must be taken care of through Iraqi resources. The Iraqis have provided the very best care possible with the tools they have available. They just don't have additional materials and personnel required to help him in his current condition.

Are you really in this battle for hearts and minds, gentlemen? Your battlefield metrics delineating how many JAM members were killed and how many ISF soldiers abandoned their posts are meaningless. We rolled out the red carpet for a JAM gunman who very well may have shot a hero who took a bullet for his country.

We Did It

Well, we did it. We got one kid out. Six months of effort, hundreds of e-mails, thousands of dollars, and now we've done it. We helped one child whom I have never met, and whom I will likely never meet, regain the use of his hands. And now we've restored vision for ten more children in almost no time at all.

I am going to do everything I can to take something positive out of this, though I have to admit right now I feel spent. I am disappointed, too, though I can't explain why. While I don't want to dwell on the negatives, I just can't help but feel overwhelmed at times by how much effort goes into so little "progress" here.

I think what I am reacting to is the fact that there hasn't been an outpouring from companies to sponsor these kids. I can't put out any public messages or tell people truthfully about the obstacles we are running into with laws and regulations. I can't call this "Katrina on steroids" without risking being put into Leavenworth. So I am left to push a neutered message that ends up sounding more like propaganda bullshit than what I want to say.

John and I are two junior officers and we did this when everyone thought it was impossible. Where the fuck are the senior officers? Where the fuck are the people who started this war?

So, I'm sorry. Yes, I am happy—very happy— that a little boy may be able to save his hands and learn something decent about this world. And now ten children will be able to see something beautiful in this world again. But I am bitterly disappointed and afraid that superiors above the division don't think this is very important. Without institutional support for this program, these children may very well heal up just well enough to join the marauding herds outside our base who are lobbing grenades at us right now.

After Dr. Akpek's mission was complete, we turned to another volunteer who had contacted us months earlier when we first sent messages to academic centers. Jorge Lazareff, a neurosurgeon from UCLA's Mattel Children's Hospital, agreed to take a trip into Kurdistan to treat children there. Dr. Lazareff and an anesthesiologist, Dr. Van de Wiele, traveled into Kurdistan without any kind of security convoy. Although it would take many more months to complete the process to get them into Kurdistan, it was amazing to see what they accomplished when it finally happened. The two physicians initiated care for over a dozen children with various complex neurosurgical conditions. They also met with health officials in the Kurdish region to start to build bridges with their offices.

To this day I'm not sure how Dr. Lazareff or Dr. Van de Wiele managed to get in and out of Kurdistan without running into significant difficulty with security issues. When I finally had the opportunity to speak with them on the phone some time later, it was apparent that they had the same impression of the clinicians that I had in my sector. The medical teams not only knew what they were doing, they were overcoming incredibly difficult obstacles to provide care to their patients. Interference from Westerners was counterproductive. Cooperating on cases the Iraqi authorities decided on, and cooperating in terms that they determined, was the most promising way to build common understanding between the two sides.

* * *

Shortly after Dr. Lazareff's trip a special forces medic, Sergeant Sam E[7], contacted us when he came across a three-year old girl named Adeela[8] who had been terribly maimed in a blast. Adeela's injuries were horrific and disturbing. Her

---

[7] Name modified for privacy
[8] Name modified for privacy

arm was so severely burned it, in effect, had melted down to scar permanently against her chest. She also was unable to chew food because her mouth and face were so badly damaged.

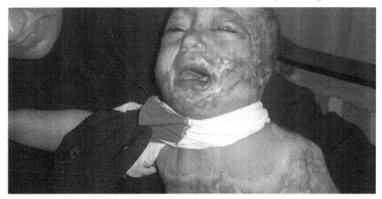

After months of processing visa paperwork with Sergeant E, we were able to evacuate Adeela to Dartmouth Hitchcock Medical Center. Dr. Mitch Stotland, Dr. Butterly, President Wright, Dean Kennedy, Rabbi Borazz, and many other people at Dartmouth went to incredible lengths to help Adeela overcome her injuries. She required nearly ten months of treatment, and two incredibly generous souls, Nahid Tabatabai and Amin Plaisted, opened their home to Adeela and her mother for that entire time.

Nahid and Amin changed their whole lives, from adding a car seat to their car to handling endless medical errands and appointments to make Adeela's care possible. They drove her round-trip to the hospital on countless occasions and helped her with her outpatient medication regimen. They also coordinated an endless number of travel arrangements, including making major road trips to pick her up on her arrival in Boston and driving all the way to New York City for her flight home. Adeela's cultural situation was also quite challenging, as she likely had some form of PTSD from the horrors she had suffered.

A road trip of that length with any two-year-old is challenging enough, let alone a child who is terrified of everything around her. Nahid and Amin deserve a special place in heaven for what they did to help Adeela.

Adeela's care occurred in the middle of the worst economic downturn in decades, including multimillion-dollar cuts to the college and hospital budgets. The officials at Dartmouth never once asked us to help with funds to offset the cost of her care. Words can't tell you how proud it made me that the Dartmouth community rescued Adeela. They transformed her life and enabled her to regain use of the arm that had been scarred down into her chest.

After countless hours and an incredible amount of time and energy building the foundation, we were finally at the point where it could really take off if we could get any kind of institutional buy-in—or even simply some public awareness. We needed an employee, or perhaps a small office. Most importantly, we needed to be able to reward donors and recruit funds without having to fear professional retribution. By the time John and I were finally preparing to return to America, I thought we would have any number of new luxuries to help us out: working telephones, e-mail, clean water, electricity, roads that didn't spontaneously erupt in explosions—you name it. But despite all the advantages we would have when we returned home, we also had a major disadvantage. We were going back to separate bases. John was staying with the infantry unit, and I was going back to the base at Walter Reed. I didn't fully appreciate it at the time, but I was heading back under the thumbs of REMFs. I was heading back to Washington, and a base full of senior leaders who know little about the reality of war.

CHAPTER 15
THE POGUE PALACE

John and I went our separate ways shortly before I left on a convoy for Kuwait. He had to stay back an extra ten days, and I have to admit, that felt to both of us like it would be another eternity. We smoked a cigar on base and toasted two nonalcoholic beers to life back in America. As I watched giant airplanes circling into the tarmac at BIAP it was somewhat surreal to think that was my ticket out of the vortex. It is so much simpler when a war zone is described on TV—almost as if you could just walk there on a long hiking trip. Sitting watching the "freedom birds" coming in and out of the sky, I was awestruck by both the amazing complexity and simplicity of it all. It was just a simple airplane. Yet, as far as I was concerned, it was a miracle. It was my ticket to the other side of the globe. I couldn't help but wonder if fighters in ancient armies felt the same way when they saw their ocean vessels pull into harbor. The airplanes were my only connection to the world, and I couldn't wait to get on one.

After traveling for days through customs, convoys, and countless layovers, we made our way to Germany. The first thing I noticed was how colorful and clean everything seemed to be. There was no dirt anywhere to be seen. And the airport terminal had more candy and snacks to eat than I could believe. They all had colorful clean wrappers, and they were surrounded by vending machines that were stocked full of cold, fresh, bubbling soda and beer.

As far as I could tell, I was in heaven.

We touched down in Bangor, Maine, as our first stop in America, and a group of Vietnam Veterans stood late into the night to shake our hands. I choked back my emotions as one of them shook my hand, stating simply, "Welcome home, soldier." He knew what was on the other side of the world, and he understood it. I hugged the hell out of him, not even knowing who he was. "Feels good, don't it?" was all he needed to say. I nodded my head in agreement, swallowing hard to keep back the tears that were filling my eyes. We were back in America. *Fuck yeah*.

After another couple stops we finally touched down at the arrival ceremony at Ft. Campbell. My parents and my in-laws were there to welcome me home, and my wife and two-year-old daughter were the first two I saw in the arrival pavilion. I couldn't believe how big my little girl had grown. I wanted to hug her forever. She wasn't too sure about the strange guy who was hugging her Mommy, but after we got some coloring books out we were back to being best friends.

Over the next several days it became apparent that none of the administrators at Ft. Campbell had any idea who I was, and likewise, nobody at Walter Reed had any idea how I was supposed to get back to Washington. So we packed up our things and headed up to my wife's rental unit in Michigan. Over the ensuing weeks we moved our family back to DC, and I made plans to start back at Walter Reed. I was ecstatic just to be back in America, and as the New Year approached, I was flying high and loving life.

* * *

My first day back at Walter Reed, I was immediately caught off guard by something that I had never even noticed before my deployment. It is an utterly unremarkable detail on a soldier's uniform, but it is more critical than any words can ever really say. It speaks volumes that civilians and others outside the infantry will never be able to fully appreciate. I now look for it immediately when I see a man in uniform—I look first for the combat patch. A combat patch is worn on the right shoulder of a uniform for Army veterans who have been to combat, and it means everything to men who have earned the right to wear it. Better yet, two small, pin-on badges, the combat infantry badge (CIB) and the combat action badge (CAB), can be worn by soldiers who have been engaged in various forms of conflict outside the wire. Altogether, these insignia can only be earned by those who have been to war and witnessed it firsthand.

When I first returned to Walter Reed, I was stunned to see how many full bird colonels were walking around in uniform with no combat patch on their right shoulders. They literally looked naked to me. In an infantry unit, a full bird colonel with no combat patch would be laughed off base. Yet at Walter Reed, it was the norm. Physicians earn a considerable amount of rank just by virtue of their education and training in school. Many physicians fresh out of fellowship training outrank battalion commanders who have had significant combat leadership experience. Physicians can be promoted for book smarts with no frontline experience. Worse yet, they are often rewarded for serving their own career interests rather than the interests of their soldiers and patients. It creates a self-serving dynamic that at times is untenable. The more I tried to readjust to life and work in America, the more untenable this reality became for me.

After I returned to Walter Reed, I was contemplating what I should do for my next job. I had the opportunity to interview at the Office of the Surgeon General for a unique position that was a significant career advancement opportunity. I was excited to think about what it might entail, and as I drove down to the Office of the Surgeon General for a job interview, it felt like I was finally arriving someplace significant in my life. I parked my car and walked into a series of massive, pristine corporate high-rises. One building had "SAIC" written across the top in giant bold letters. I wondered for a moment if anybody in the office at Science Applications International Corporation realized that I was the low-ranking officer who sent a fundraising challenge to their headquarters almost a year earlier. Judging from the size of this one building, representing just a small portion of their total enterprise, I didn't think my anonymity was threatened in any way.

As I strolled through the hallways in my dress uniform, I tried not to stare at the decorative fountains and glistening floors. I had been in this kind of environment before, but now somehow it all looked so unusual to me. It was all so clean. It was all so new. It was all so colorful. It was all so completely unremarkable to the men walking around in their suits and ties.

I was greeted by a security guard who addressed me by name and directed me to the correct elevator for my visit. The security guard was carrying a rather sad-looking 9-mm pistol in his rusted holster, which seemed oddly out of place—especially with a magazine already loaded in it. I was taken rather quickly back to the last time I saw my loaded 9-mm magazine on FOB Justice. The Office of the Surgeon General was just like FOB Justice, only it didn't have porta-shitters, incoming rockets, or bloody entrails from dead casualties parked in a cargo bin outside. I could see how someone might confuse the two and opt to carry a rusted-out 9-mm handgun—never know when a suicide bomber might sneak up on you in suburban Virginia.

As I headed up in the elevators, I tried to keep the new-job jitters to a minimum by reminding myself that I wasn't naïve about how this kind of office world worked. I had been in surroundings like this before. I had seen the corporate recruiters from Goldmans Sachs and McKinsey come host dinners for students at Dartmouth. My crew team had competed in the Ivy League Championships, and many of my buddies even competed in the Royal Henley Regatta in England. When their parents took us out to lunch in highbrow restaurants, they would talk about labor relations at their international manufacturing plants in Taiwan. Either that, or they would ask us about our quantum mechanics classes and cross-industry applications for financial engineering. I had been an audience to high society before and found ways to blend in. So this time around I didn't have to furrow my brow in disbelief or drop my jaw to the floor looking around like a fool.

But I did.

At first I thought the luxurious surroundings were distracting, but that wasn't what really threw me so far off. Hell, even the luxury of a grocery store had seemed strange to me when I first got back to America. What got to me was something else. Unfortunately, the more and more senior officers I saw upstairs in the high-rise, the worse and worse it got.

The senior generals and officers walking all around me didn't have combat patches. I had grown up idolizing these men as the leaders of our country. In my mind they represented the very best in medicine, and the very best in military leadership. They were supposed to uphold and embody the meaning of selfless service to our country and to humanity. Yet they had sent my friends off to war when they themselves had never been there. They had never probed layers of flesh blown apart on their buddies, or witnessed the horrific civilian disasters that are an inevitable part of war. They had not borne the burden that almost a decade of war had created. All of them had the benefits of illustrious and successful military careers that were developed without experiencing any kind of trauma in war. I was stunned. Dumbfounded. Speechless.

How do you set the medical rules of engagement if you don't know what war looks like? How can you lead our wounded warriors if you've never consoled, treated, even simply talked with one of our fighters inside the war zone? How do you allocate resources for post-traumatic stress disorder if you've never seen a friend die in a blast?

Every time I had ever been on a team in my life, the leaders in the locker room were the guys who worked hardest and took the hits for the team. Here, the exact opposite was true. The people who had found ways to serve their own interests had risen to the top, and the men I knew who had taken hits for the team—well, they were in body bags or breathing on ventilators.

I went on to interview with a lieutenant colonel who ran the department with the new potential job assignment. During the interview, the lieutenant colonel asked me a question that I had never been asked before. He turned to me and asked, "Jon, are you a tactical or a strategic thinker?"

In retrospect, I had no idea just how profound a moment that was, even if the question at the time struck me as rather bizarre. I had been focusing so intently on diverting my stare away from all the combat patch–less right shoulders around me that I barely understood his question. I didn't know what he was driving at, so I did my best to offer an articulate but noncommittal answer.

The connotations that are hidden in that question are critical though, and they strike at the core of the mindset for leaders in the Beltway who have never seen combat. I didn't realize it myself for another year after the interview, but it was my first introduction to the kind of bullshit that has infected our foreign policy leaders at every level. The rest of the day at the Office of the Surgeon General was uneventful, but over the course of the next year I would come to develop a firsthand appreciation for the underlying motive behind the colonel's question.

* * *

Inside policy circles in Washington, it is expected that true leaders are "strategic" thinkers. Unlike common folk, such strategic thinkers are especially gifted. They are able to rise above the noisy din of combat chaos to set a grander vision for the American empire in the arc of history. Strategic thinkers are fond of grandiose posturing, academic theories and other assorted forms of hubris that are used to frame the historical context and justification for war. Picture a diplomat sipping on cognac, having a fireside chat with international dealer-brokers. A pinkie in the air and a perfectly adorned suit offer the intellectual backdrop to assert that his grandiose vision of the world is what truly smart and capable people think. Everyone knows that war is the natural state of man, and strategic thinkers are there to shape and mold their egos around its shining, benevolent carnage. It just so happens that strategic thinkers are not only full of themselves, but also full of shit.

Don't get me wrong, there are compelling academic theories and policy ideas that make strategic thinking sound appealing at face value—otherwise the ideas would gain no traction in leadership circles. Strategically speaking, Iraq is the "global commons" for the world. Ever since Britain drew up boundaries after World War I, policy experts have argued over the best way to distribute and share its resources. Strategically speaking, fair and transparent markets are the most efficient way to maximize the value of those resources for Iraq and the world. The alternative is to empower a dictatorial madman like Saddam Hussein, which leaves no alternative but to intervene and establish fair markets. The same sort of overarching strategic narrative can be applied to Afghanistan, a geographically priceless location that triangulates the Russian, Persian, and Chinese empires. The "Silk Road" for global trade crosses right through Afghanistan, and it has been part of conflicts since Alexander the Great and Ghengis Khan.

The problem is our national strategic objectives are being set by senior personnel who have no idea what tactical issues exist at the ground level of war. As a result, there is a gaping chasm between our foreign policy strategic vision and the tactical realities involved in implementing it. That gaping chasm includes deeply held religious and cultural values that are completely antithetical to foreign interference, no matter what strategic rationale is used. The result on a tactical level is not surprising: mass chaos, bloodshed, and never-ending rivalries for power.

While I can certainly appreciate the need for higher-level approaches to management problems, it is all too easy for elitist strategic thinking to become an incestuous and self-perpetuating infection for our leaders. The appeal for power has caused our leaders to lose touch not only with tactical realities but more importantly with the truly compelling strategic problems for our country. A "big-picture" strategic analysis would show that our obsession with foreign policy has come at the expense of domestic policies to rebuild our own nation. Strategic thinkers have been high on their foreign policy horses for more than a decade now, and they have ignored domestic policies that impact our country every day.

Tactical thinking, much like domestic policy, gets short shrift inside the Beltway because it is "for operational people" or for grunts to figure out. How do we keep our enemies from blowing apart our soldiers? I don't know. Don't we have some tactical thinkers who like to muddle around in such mundane details? You are asking me about food and water supply lines for our forward assets? Oh, bother, don't we have some hired hands around here who can deal with such a low-level matter? Can't you see I am busy charting a course for our empire through the arc of history?

Tactical thinking is what soldiers who are fighting for survival have to rely upon day in and day out. It is absolutely essential, and invariably the only truly transformative policy strategies emerge from tactical experience in the trenches. Ideas that are born amid the cruel and vicious realities of tactical experience are what hold the power to change the world. They are battle tested and grounded in a foundation of frontline experience.

Despite the critical importance of tactical knowledge, it is scoffed at by higher levels of command in exactly the same manner that manual labor is scoffed at by the executive suite.

While the leaders in the executive suite can do whatever they want for a long period of time, eventually what is happening in the trenches will come back to haunt them if they fail to lead from the front. Executives who don't get off their thrones and lead in the trenches will get what they deserve, even if it takes years for the rot in the roots to reach the branches at the top.

Strategic thinking and tactical thinking cannot be separated. While they may have different lanes, neither one can survive without the other. As Sun Tzu put it in *Art of War*, "Tactics without strategy is the noise before defeat. Strategy without tactics is the slowest route to victory." Leaders who understand tactical realities and integrate them into their strategic policy visions make the best long-term decisions.

As I spent more and more time inside policy think-tank circles, I came to appreciate that many federal foreign policy institutions are full of people who are high on strategic thinking with no tactical basis for their opinions. It is so much cooler, after all, to be a "high-level" strategic thinker about foreign affairs. As a result, senior-level leaders who don't have combat experience are being groomed into positions with massive responsibilities and incredible privilege without any experiential foundation whatsoever.

I don't make this assertion lightly, as it lies at the crux of what has become our foreign policy and ongoing wars. Foreign policy strategy has become the way to advance your career in the Beltway, and it has come at the expense of the plain vanilla homework involved in crafting solid domestic policy. Which one is more interesting to you: signals intelligence and covert operations, or figuring out how to regulate a bank or school? The answer is obvious. I'll take one helping of James Bond, please. Unfortunately, while power-hungry careerists run around with a hard-on looking for sexy Bond chicks, the banks, schools, and infrastructure of our country are facing unprecedented challenges.

There is an entire community of professional academics who wander around Washington aggressively branding themselves as strategic visionaries in order to develop their careers. Plain faculty appointments in urban planning or civil engineering are so passé. These days anyone with any real career aspirations knows that the best way to enter the "flag-grade" stratosphere is to leverage your PhD in some type of national security issue. Once you have that in place, you declare your loyalty to either the Democrat or Republican tribe and join one of their "nonpartisan" think tanks. Once you land that gig you can publish academic policy "white papers" that hold all the legitimacy of a nonpartisan organization. Of course, the nonpartisan organization you join is the best way to advance your connections within the partisan tribe at the cocktail party du jour.

What does this mean outside Washington? *It's simple: more reasons for war, so long as someone else is fighting it.* So long as you avoid the messy realities of actually living in the combat situations that your "white paper" suggests, you've done your job. If you want extra credit, you can take a field trip to the combat zone to shake hands on a CODEL (congressional delegation) or other VIP trip, and then speak with far more expertise than a two-week vacation ought to earn you. For a perfect example of this, just look at Michael O'Hanlon and other "talking heads" from the Brookings Institution. Dr. O'Hanlon was everywhere in 2007, indicating that the Iraq war was transformed after he had a chance to visit the country. That idiot was in Iraq on a two-week vacation, yet every major media outlet put him on television to speak as if he was the world's leading expert on the subject. Three years later, in 2010, he was back at it, arguing that he was an expert on Afghanistan. Never mind the fact that he was working for a think tank that was funded directly by major defense and oil interests. The guy is a PhD. Would a PhD ever whore out his academic credentials to ingratiate himself to the powerful Wizard of Oz who is paying the bills behind the curtain?

General Eisenhower issued a warning about this phenomenon decades ago. He advised America that the very real need for a standing military would also require an extensive and self-serving industry that comes with it. He warned everyone that the individual career interests of those in power would eventually overpower the interests of our frontline soldiers and our citizens. As far as I can tell, he was profoundly—almost prophetically—correct.

Nine years of continuous war with an all-volunteer Army has created a situation where very few members of our ruling elite, or their family members, have paid any burden to society. As a result, government leaders and their parallel academic policy and industry advisors have represented their own strategic interests at the expense of the tactical interests of our frontline soldiers. If your career is advanced by promulgating war at someone else's expense, the result is not that surprising. There are notable exceptions of course—Senator Kerry, Senator McCain, Senator Webb, Representative Patrick Murphy, and Beau Biden to name a few. But they are the laudable and remarkable exceptions, rather than the rule.

A few years after the colonel at the surgeon general's office first asked me about strategic thinking, I experienced what I believe is the quintessential example of how far awry this phenomenon has gone. I had the good fortune to be chosen for a National Security Fellowship inside one of the policy think tank organizations I spoke about inside Washington. It is a new think tank full of veterans who have worked very hard to overhaul our energy and national security policies in simple, pragmatic ways. It is also closely aligned with the Democratic tribe, though fellows do not have to declare a loyalty to the party in order to be selected. (I will say, though, I haven't met a Republican at any of the cocktail parties yet.)

As part of the fellowship, they arranged meetings for us inside the secretary of defense's office with several of the deputy assistant secretaries of defense ("DASDs" or "daz-dees," as they are known by the cool kids). The meetings were designed to help us understand more about how high-level policy decisions are made.

DASDs hold significant budgetary and decision-making authority in our world. During the fellowship trip, I had a chance to meet with one, or it may have been "just" the DASDs chief of staff. Whoever he was, he was so much more powerful than me that he didn't need to dwell on his official title. He had a corner office in the top ring of the Pentagon, and it was evident he was in the club that ran the show. He was responsible for managing the arms sales arrangements with several preeminent Middle Eastern gulf states, including Saudi Arabia, the UAE, and other allies.

Judging by his appearance, I think he was about my age, in his early to mid thirties. He was not married and he did not have children. He had never served in the military. He was a former McKinsey consultant who was appointed to his post after serving on a political campaign. All those things are fine and dandy—a bit surprising, but fine and dandy. McKinsey has some really sharp people and I'm sure he is smart enough to get up to speed and really sink his teeth into his new job. He had to be, as he managed a portfolio that included hundreds of billions of dollars in advanced weapons sales.

We were informally sharing some doughnuts in a group of about ten "strategic thinkers" when he mentioned the progress he had been making on weapons programs inside the DoD. He had been a part of the team that reduced the F-22 fighter budget. It was a surprise to many people inside the Beltway when a program like that actually faced budget cuts. It was interesting that he had assessed whether the program was needed, rather than simply grow his budget request to gain power.

He then cracked a joke, saying that maybe the Pentagon could use the money it saved on the F-22 to help our frontline guys win hearts and minds instead. Thinking he was being sarcastic about the hearts and minds mantra, I laughingly agreed. And then with my big mouth full of doughnuts, I blurted out, "Yeah, I bet every eleven bravo would just love to have his own F-22 to help him win those hearts and minds!" Every eleven bravo (combat infantryman) that I know would love to have his own fighter jet to destroy his enemies en masse. That way, the hearts and minds that are splattered on the sidewalk are all in total agreement with his perspective. If you don't believe me, just ask pancake man.

That is probably disturbing for most civilians to hear, but I've yet to know an eleven bravo infantryman who didn't find the hearts and mind discourse to be a canned bunch of bullshit. That isn't the main point of the story, though—the point of this story is how the DASD responded. He immediately turned to me with a confused look and stammered something that made it clear we weren't on the same wavelength. Having been trained to be reflexively terrified of any authority figure, I tried not to let the surprise show on my face as I choked down my doughnut. Desperately stalling for time with powder conspicuously smeared all over my lips, I realized I was fucked. The DASD continued to address me, and as he did, it slowly became obvious why we were having an uncomfortable exchange. *Holy shit,* I realized. *He doesn't know what a fucking eleven bravo is.*

I felt like I was in one of those old Southwest Airlines commercials where the sound goes "bing" and the voice asks, "Want to get away"? Um, yes, please. There is no way for me to participate in this awkward interlude without offending a far more powerful person across the table from me. Actually, could I borrow one of the shelved F-22s to get me out of this office as fast as fucking possible?

In my foolish excitement to be talking with someone inside the Office of the Secretary of Defense, I had completely failed to filter my comments. Everyone had said that the meeting was among friends and strictly off the record. I didn't think it would be *that* far off the record.

What's an eleven bravo? How the fuck do I answer that? Here is one of the top ten decision makers at the Pentagon. A deputy assistant secretary of defense or his chief of staff doesn't know how to refer to a fucking infantryman? That's like a doctor not knowing what a stethoscope is. How the fuck do you become a DASD or chief of staff without knowing what an eleven bravo is?

I don't care if you're the smartest person on earth. If you don't know what an eleven bravo is (or an O-311 in the Marines) then you shouldn't be making "strategic" decisions about war. Period. The end. Fuck you, go back to square one. Go live in the tactical shit for a bit and get your hands dirty with blood. Then maybe the fifty billion dollars' worth of weapons you just sold in the Middle East will look a little different to you.

CHAPTER 16
NEVER STAND BETWEEN A CANNIBAL AND HIS DINNER

One day I was covering emergency duties at an undisclosed, non-military location when one of the country's senior-most leaders was brought to me with a serious problem. Out of a personal sense of loyalty to him, and for obvious legal reasons, I want to be careful to maintain complete privacy pertaining to his circumstances. I hope this senior leader can forgive me for even broaching the subject of our interaction obliquely, but the words of advice he relayed to me after our encounter have come to lie at the center of the moral fabric for my life. I would be selfish and untrue to my brothers in arms if I did not share the words of wisdom that he ultimately imparted to me that day.

The senior leader had a potentially lethal condition that was very serious but didn't require immediate surgical intervention. I assessed him and initiated some stabilizing measures that alleviated the immediate urgency of his problem. In doing so, I spoke with him and performed a physical exam. Unfortunately for both of us, his physical exam had to include a rather personal and intimate interaction that was, shall we say, excessively uncomfortable for both of us. A personal exam is always awkward, but when it is a senior leader, it is also strangely terrifying. Everybody hates to have their ass crack hanging out of a gown. When it's a senior leader, well, what can I say? Our national figures are humans, too.

I had long before made a habit of asking senior leaders for their advice as I examined them so I could set myself a bit more at ease. I loved to hear what they had to say about their work, and I loved to learn from the lessons they had experienced over the years. It was such an incredible privilege to be able to have personal time with men and women like that, and this gentleman was a very kind mentor who offered up his insights on life as well.

After I completed my exam, I sat and listened to the guidance he had to offer, and it was fascinating to hear. I have to admit I was thrown a little bit off guard the first time he referred to one of his subordinate protégés by his first name. His protégé was a public figure who was on television quite regularly, and I tried rather desperately not to let the shock on my face show when I heard him refer to this man on a first-name basis. Eventually I got to the point where I just nodded my head in agreement with his stories, as if hearing Admiral Smith[9] referred to as "Bob" was something I heard every day. Even typing that sentence makes me cringe, as if my utterly revolting insubordination can come echoing off this page.

I remember the advice the senior leader offered quite clearly. He told me that inside Washington, everyone will

---

[9] Name changed because I am physically incapable of performing the number of push-ups that would be required if "Admiral Smith" ever knew I referred to him as "Bob"

smile at you and congratulate you on whatever efforts you are undertaking in your work. "Ten out of ten" people will offer you collegial praise and encouragement. The trick, he told me, was that "nine out of ten mean it." And through the complex laws of deductive reasoning, he obviously meant that there was always one left over who wasn't really on your side. He went on to tell me, "You have to figure out who that person is because they are trying to knife you in the back or steal the food from your plate."

It was pretty sobering advice. We went on to talk a bit further and I told him about some of my experiences treating soldiers who had been blown up in Iraq. At that point he looked at me and asked me, "Doc, have you ever seen me talking on television?" I was embarrassed to admit I hadn't, and I scrambled a bit to blame it on the fact I hardly ever watch television with our young children at home. He could sense I felt embarrassed and quickly interjected, "No, Doc, don't worry. I know you haven't seen me speaking on television because I won't ever appear on television." I couldn't sense what exactly he was driving at, so I sat and listened in silence. He continued, "I was offered seven million dollars to leave my position and appear on network television. I turned down the offer."

While senior flag grade leaders make a perfectly comfortable salary after decades in public service, they are anything but rich. In fact, I would venture a guess that most junior physicians like myself earn slightly more than this leader, even though he had nearly thirty years in public service. A multimillion-dollar offer would be a life-changing event for him and for his family. He could see I had raised my eyebrows, knowing that such a huge sum would have a transformative impact not only on him but also on his children and grandchildren.

I sat there listening patiently, feeling as if I were hearing the deathbed confession of a man looking over the entire history of his life. In a way, that was what he was sharing with me. I was stunned to be in the position I was in, hearing words of amazing clarity that he obviously was not filtering or guarding in any way. He was offering his most candid insights on what principles he held most sacred throughout his life.

The television contract was clearly an important issue for him, and one that seemed to go far beyond the significant financial ramifications. He was getting at something else, so I asked him, "Why did you turn them down, sir?" He paused for a long time, clearly struggling to find the right words to impart how important this issue was to him.

"I didn't want to throw our men under the bus. I will not be a cannibal."

That answer will stick with me to my grave. While it probably sounds abstract for anyone who works outside of a structured chain of command, it painted a crystal-clear picture to me. It offered the perfect analogy for how the world works inside Washington. Life there is seen as a never-ending contest, and the name of the game is to claw and scratch your way up the food chain of power no matter what the consequences are— or who pays them. Up until that point in time I hadn't really been able to describe this phenomenon succinctly to my friends outside the military or federal government. Now, this leader had just given me the perfect description for the game and the competition involved. The name of the game is "may the best cannibal win," and in its most sick and twisted form it involves throwing your subordinates into the meat grinder of war in order to advance your own career and personal rewards.

Allow me to put a concrete example around this cannibalism analogy so it doesn't sound so abstract. Flag grade leaders (both civilian and military) receive an annual salary just under two hundred thousand dollars without any equity incentives, stock options, or other means to build wealth. While two hundred thousand dollars is certainly a handsome salary, it takes thirty years of total dedication to the institution to rise to that level—and by total dedication, I mean subjugating all things to the needs of the government for thirty years. That includes everything related to your family and the stability of your household even when we're not in an active war. In my opinion, two hundred thousand dollars is a gross underpayment for the responsibilities a flag grade leader must handle, even taking into consideration that they will retire with a government pension. Once a flag grade leader retires, he collects smaller monthly pension disbursements that, again, provide a perfectly handsome income to live on quite comfortably. However, the federal pension pales in comparison to the payday a flag grade leader collects if he "sells out" to the career interests inside Washington, such as the defense and lobbying industries.

When they retire, flag grade leaders field offers from massive multinational companies who are eager to have senior leadership on their board of directors. Many other political officials make a habit of doing this in what is known as the revolving door in Washington. They come into town, work for a few years in a position inside the government, and then take a private sector job that leverages their experience and contacts inside the government. Their private sector work often doubles or triples their pay, and it almost invariably involves inside knowledge they gain while working in the government. As a result, one of the major incentives public officials have while in office is to position themselves to maximize the private sector payout they can collect when they are done.

Since senior flag grade leaders don't have the same private sector opportunities on the way up their career ladders, the bonuses that are dangled in front of them when they retire are all the more impressive. The money can often dwarf their entire public sector career earnings. As a result, generals, admirals, and other senior civilian SES (senior executive service) leaders are faced with a profoundly challenging conflict of interest. Known as "agency-principal discordance" in executive management parlance, it is the same kind of moral hazard that the CEOs in major investment banks exploited in the lead up to the financial crisis. That is to say, their own personal interests are only advanced if they make decisions that inflict harm on their own men.

Leaders who stand on principle and decline payments from the defense and lobbying industry are often portrayed to be loners who have dared to question the military-security fraternity. Yet soldiers of all ranks know that the rare leaders who take such a stand are the only true leaders in the fraternity. They are the exceptional men who have the courage to forego personal privilege based solely on principle. They refuse, at a great expense to themselves, not to cannibalize their subordinates. I know who they are, and the men I fought with know who they are. *They are the leaders and guardians of our country.* They stand ready to fight anytime it is necessary, but they are also disciplined and principled enough not to seek out war for their own personal profit and benefit.

The leader I took care of that day turned down the multimillion-dollar television contract, and he was very discerning in selecting what business ventures he pursued in the private sector. He refused to cannibalize his men by glorifying war on television, and he refused to accept the payouts to run a firm that profited from war. Almost all of his peers have accepted massive sums of money to promote wars in which their subordinates have been killed. They are being paid to be cannibals who profit from the blood of their own men, and it is sickening. It is a transformation that is antithetical to generations of American leadership principles.

Countless senior members of the civilian and military policy apparatus have taken advantage of this morally repugnant leadership failure for almost a decade now. All the while, the Joint Theater Trauma Registry (JTTR) that tracks injuries from the Iraq and Afghanistan wars has shown that *only one flag-grade leader has ever been injured from the fighting*. Tragically, and with rather awful irony, that officer was actually trying to get Doctors Without Borders into remote parts of Afghanistan when he was wounded.

One could make the argument that this is not new, of course. As the saying goes, old men talk of war and young men die in war. The conflict of interest that war creates has been discussed throughout human history, perhaps most notably by Plato in ancient Greece. Plato argued passionately that members of the guardian class in society must be insulated from the temptations of gold. Just like in ancient Greece, this issue is of critical importance for our country today. As Plato wrote:

> *He who is to be a noble guardian of the State will require to unite in himself philosophy and spirit and swiftness and strength...All that belongs to them, should be such as will neither impair their virtue*

as guardians, nor tempt them to prey upon the other citizens.

And they alone of all the citizens may not touch or handle silver or gold, or be under the same roof with them, or wear them, or drink from them. And this will be their salvation, and they will be the saviours of the State.

But should they ever acquire moneys of their own, they will become enemies and tyrants instead of allies of the other citizens...Therefore, we must enquire who are the best guardians of their own conviction. (Plato, The Republic, II-IV, 135)

The senior national leader who was offered the television contract faced temptations that are exactly the same as the ones our civilian policy leaders face. Our politicians are paid, just like he was paid, to keep the defense contracts flowing. The Democratic Party received $12.2 million from the top defense industry donors and political action committees (PACs) in the 2008 election cycle. The Republican Party received $11.6 million from the top donors and PACs in the same year. Both of these totals are above and beyond the $150.8 million that registered defense lobbyists spent on those same federal officials that year. In aggregate, the defense lobbyists paid an average of $26,500 to each of the 435 congressmen in the House of Representatives ($24,800 per Republican, $28,100 per Democrat). Each of the hundred senators was paid an average of $64,150 ($65,600 per Democrat, $62,700 per Republican).

These sums don't even touch on the influence of the oil and energy companies that have benefited from the wars. They contributed $77.7 million in election PAC donations and $389.2 million in lobbying contributions in 2008. On average, that translated to $54,950 per congressman and $201,350 per senator. The best senators for each party took in approximately $550,000 each from oil and energy interests. Senator Lisa Murkowski, a Republican from Alaska, raked in $557,672. Senator Blanche Lincoln, a Democrat from Arkansas, managed to collect $548,296. I'm sure there is a pithy comment on bipartisan cooperation to be found in there somewhere, but somehow it is eluding me.[10]

In addition to the PACs, there are 527 groups and other entities—even "non-individual 'persons'"—who pay congresspeople to keep the war machine rolling. So long as your child isn't the one being cannibalized in the war, you have no incentive to stop the insanity. Anyone who might consider interrupting the process will only be portrayed as cowards who are "soft" on national security. The truth, of course, is that the lowliest cowards are the cannibals at the trough.

I fully understand that this is the way of the world, and the way of our country. There are times when war is an essential and vital reality for our society. It has solved slavery, fascism, and arguably communism as well. I also understand that the world is a big, dark jungle full of carnivores competing for resources in life. But being a carnivore is different from being a cannibal. I will compete and fight with the best carnivores on the planet to protect my country and provide for my family. But I will never be a cannibal.

---

[10] Source:http://www.opensecrets.org/industries/indus.php?ind=D&goButt2.x=12&goButt2.y=5

In his famous "military industrial congressional complex" speech, General Eisenhower highlighted the dangers of the cannibalization phenomenon. General Eisenhower was the last great president who was not afraid to stand between the cannibals and their dinner. He was not afraid to protect the men who served underneath him from congressmen, generals, admirals, SES executives, corporate executives, academics, think-tanks, and other senior leaders who are heavily incentivized to promote war. General Eisenhower made certain that if he asked his soldiers to go to war, there was a compelling reason for it, and he made certain that his decisions were not colored by his own financial incentives. He knew war from the inside out, and as a former combat leader, he understood exactly what it entails. That is precisely why his men would follow him through hell and back, and fight to the death on his behalf.

I've watched too many idealistic young men die before me to just ride along and keep my mouth shut. I refuse to simply cash my check and rise up the food chain of power. I doubt any of the men in my death bin had any idea that such perverse personal and financial incentives exist for our modern leaders. So, on their behalf, I would just like to say those things that are never actually said to the power hungry cannibals in Washington: Fuck you very much, Sir. Fuck you very, very much.

CHAPTER 17
ETHICS

It wasn't long before I found myself walking in my dress uniform again, heading down another long, ornate hallway. The fundraising challenge John and I issued to the defense industry contractors had found its way into the *Boston Globe*, and we had managed to evacuate another child for surgery. I had hoped the Army might take an interest in this child, and since I was finally stateside, I had asked a new public affairs officer if he might consider writing an article about her case. I thought his office could help highlight what our frontline guys had done to get her out of harm's way.

Prior to talking with public affairs, I had passed up the issue through my chain of command at Walter Reed as previously instructed, though I knew the chain of command at Walter Reed didn't really understand what we had built in Iraq. Since many leaders at Walter Reed had never been to combat, even fewer had ever stepped outside the wire. As recently as 2011, the hospital commander had never been near a war zone, and I can assure you that every soldier under his care noticed. It is beyond me how someone with zero combat experience can be put in charge of hundreds of men who have seen the most graphic trauma humankind has to offer. But, as a junior officer,

I couldn't say anything about it. So I stuck with the proper procedures and worked within the channels I was given.

I did my best to write up a detailed memo along with a brief five-slide Power Point presentation that put the project into terms drawn from the FM 3-24 counterinsurgency manual. FM 3-24 states very clearly that interagency cooperation and "synchronization of logical lines of operation (LLO)" are the cornerstones for effective foreign policy. Since the foundation John and I started was an interagency idea coming from junior levels in the military hierarchy, I had to find ways to make it appealing to my local leaders on base. Unfortunately, the REMFs in America were even more clueless about tactical realities than the REMFs in the Green Zone, so I faced an uphill battle.

John and I knew the foundation had a direct impact on mission objectives that were spelled out quite clearly by senior command in FM 3-24. But even if the foundation addressed what the senior-most levels of command in the executive suite actually wanted, that didn't really matter. What mattered were the hundreds of middle-management layers that existed between the executive suite and us. In order to navigate the hierarchy in garrison (on base), I had to find a way for the project to appeal to my bosses at Walter Reed. My goal, as far as I could tell, was to be sure the idea made my immediate superiors look good so they might consider adopting it—or at least refrain from obstructing it.

The memo I wrote up went into greater details for operational planning and integration with institutional resources than anyone at Walter Reed would readily understand; however, the Power Point slides were simple and straightforward. The way I figured it, "keep it simple, stupid" was the best way to draw support from my immediate supervisors, so I put together a series of pictures of children we had helped in the Power Point slides. If the project went up past their level, then someone with senior insights could delve into the memo I attached and see how the program could help mission critical objectives.

I submitted the Power Point presentation and the project description to the Walter Reed chain of command as directed. The long and short of it was we simply needed someone in public affairs to let us talk publicly about the foundation so we could build up more resources. Unfortunately we had already been turned down on so many occasions in so many ways—including numerous individuals in public affairs in Iraq and at Walter Reed—that it felt impossibly difficult to be starting over from scratch with a new chain of command. We had tried so many other avenues, I just put the whole project out there, hoping that someone would catch on to the potential it held to mitigate civilian trauma in combat.

A few weeks later, I was called in to receive the final legal review from a JAG lawyer who was a full bird colonel. Unfortunately I noticed immediately that he did not have a combat patch on his right shoulder. He called me into his office, and in deference to his rank, I stood at parade-rest attention. Standing still in my cleanly pressed uniform, I was trying not to be distracted by the trickling sound of the waterfall that ordained his office area. The water was sparkling clean, and it poured out next to an air-conditioner that made the mist refreshingly cool. It stood in stark contrast to the sewage that I had smelled baking in the streets of Iraq, yet there in his office it was little more than an afterthought. An afterthought, that is, for anyone who had never been bothered by the nuisance of combat.

"Jon, we can appreciate what you're trying to do here, but the fact of the matter is..."

I kept my jaw clenched shut without any expression showing on my face. I already knew what canned phrases and bullshit were sure to follow. I realized that despite my best attempts to build a project to reflect positively on Walter Reed and the military, the combat-less colonels weren't interested in what John and I had built.

I couldn't openly wish that I had my weapon again, or I would find myself locked up in a Leavenworth psych ward. That option wasn't too appealing. I didn't think it would come with built-in waterfalls. The colonel carried on, but I had long since stopped listening.

WHERE THE FUCK WAS IT?!

FUCKING GRID...GET THE FUCKING GRID!

ROCKETS—FUCK—ROCKETS!

TAMPA, ON; TAMPA, THREE DOWN COMING IN HOT!

NO, CUBS—CUBS NORTH RIGHT AT THE FUCKING GATE!

DOC, DOC, FUCKIN' EFP HIT RIGHT AT THE GATE, DOC, RIGHT AT THE FUCKING GATE!!

WE NEED MORE FUCKING MEDICS! WE NEED MORE FUCKING MEDICS!!

I stopped daydreaming about simpler times and listened as the colonel completed his monologue. "...and so you see, that is why it just wouldn't be ethical for public affairs to disclose anything about your challenge to these companies or the foundation you've created. Good luck to you."

I thanked the colonel for his time. I kept my head down like my dad had told me and did everything I could not to kill that rear-echelon motherfucker with my bare hands. After all the hurdles, after all the impossibly difficult challenges, after all the relentless bullshit, now a pogue-ass lawyer was pulling rank to squash this whole thing. And there he was telling me we couldn't ask public affairs to publish a story about the child we were currently helping, or continue challenging the defense contractor industry—*because it was unethical.*

I got into my car and just started driving. I kept driving aimlessly around the Beltway—screaming and shouting at nothing and everything at the same time. I was beside myself with anger, and given the expletives I was spewing, it was for the better that I was alone in my car. I just didn't give a fuck. I yelled at every car I passed like a psychotic sociopath. I fit right in on the Beltway.

I had my radio blaring full blast with Drowning Pool and songs by other bands we used to play downrange to fire us up. "Let the bodies hit the floor, let the bodies hit the floor, let the bodies hit the FL---OO----ORRR!" I very well may have been doing a hundred miles an hour in my shitty little Toyota. I didn't give a shit about anything or anyone.

A Johnny Cash song, "Hurt," came on, and I hit repeat. I had read about the song in a book called *Chasing Ghosts* that I had come across when we were in Kadamiyah. The book was written by Paul Rieckhoff, an infantry platoon leader who came back from combat to start the Iraq & Afghanistan Veterans Association (IAVA). He single-handedly built—from the ground up—the largest organization representing the veterans of our generation. In the book, Lieutenant Rieckhoff talks about how when he first returned to America, he just sat on the beach for weeks, listening to Johnny Cash's rendition of the song "Hurt."

I drove myself to Arlington Cemetery and parked my car. I walked up the hill past President Kennedy's grave and picked out a spot where I could sit on the grass. I had the Johnny Cash song playing on repeat in my earphones. I was sure I was violating protocol by sitting on the grass listening to headphones in my uniform, but I didn't care. I didn't give a fuck about anything. I stared out at the rows and rows of gravestones in the valley beneath me as Johnny Cash sang the last song of his life:

"You can have it all, my empire of dirt...If I could start again, my sweetest friend, I would keep myself—I would find a way."

The words in the song hit the nail on the head. I looked over at the grave next to me on the hill. It was a former chairman of the Joint Chiefs of Staff who had defended our country during a major war. I had never once heard his name. Yet, there he was lying on top of a pile of dirt in Arlington. During his life he had won the race. He had emerged on top of the food chain. Sitting there at that moment I only noticed one thing—he wasn't buried among his men in the valley below. He wasn't buried next to his wife or his children. I thought he must be pretty lonely there in eternity. I hoped for his sake that his empire of dirt was more meaningful in the afterlife than it appeared to me at that moment.

* * *

After sitting and staring for hours at the graves in the fields below me, I gathered my stuff together. I drove home, sat down, and started to figure out another way to work around the lawyer's decision. I had just started my new graduate school classes that week up at Yale. I went through my civilian e-mail account to look up information on students who were also veterans there, and I started to ask for help.

Through a friend of a friend, I found the e-mail address for a young lieutenant at "that other pretty good school in Boston." The lieutenant happened to be the son of a prominent four-star general. I decided I was going to send the lieutenant a copy of the Power Point presentation about the foundation. Technically speaking, it wasn't insubordination since I was writing from a civilian e-mail account to an officer who was not superior to my rank. But it was a huge risk to step outside my chain of command, and I was sweating bullets when I sent the message. Within hours there was an encouraging reply from the lieutenant's father, who was arguably the most prominent four-star general in the country at the time. It was a huge breakthrough that I never thought would happen.

My wife and I had a new baby at home and I had just started my new courses that week, so my e-mail account wasn't reliable at the time. It took me nearly a day and a half to download my new inbox messages, and that's when I realized the four-star general had already replied in a matter of hours to my inquiry. I read his message as the sound of *Dora the Explorer* blared from my three-year-old daughter's DVD player. I was well beyond embarrassed at my disorganized stupidity. President Kennedy once famously said in the midst of the Cuban missile crisis, "There's always some asshole who doesn't get the message." In failing to answer a four-star general for a day and a half, I was that asshole. Thankfully he was forgiving in his e-mail replies. Apparently even a four-star general understands the powers of *Dora the Explorer*.

The general was encouraging about the initiatives we had taken with the foundation, and he helped me get in touch with his senior surgeon, who was quite helpful and took the time to speak with me personally on the phone. I was very grateful for all this and completely shocked at how quickly everything moved after all the struggles John and I had run into at lower levels. Unfortunately I had rather foolishly mentioned in my original message that I had to go outside the Walter Reed chain of command to get things worked out, and I apologized for circumventing the institutional bureaucracy there. But before I could do anything to control the situation, word got back to my chain of command. My superiors were less than thrilled that I had skirted the rules and that my message had bypassed the medical chain of command entirely on its way directly up to the Pentagon. I understood their frustration with me, but by this point in time it was becoming clear I wouldn't be able to continue my schoolwork and stay on active duty anyway. If I could have solved the hurdles in a less disruptive way, I absolutely would have done so, but frankly my main concern was to keep the project alive and to help the next child get surgery.

The next time I was back at Walter Reed, I was provided with a complimentary reminder about how the chain of command is supposed to work. The Walter Reed JAG colonel contacted the Office of the Surgeon General later that week to reassure his contacts there that he had taken care of the problems I had created. To this day, I am convinced he thinks our foundation will never go any further. I kept my e-mail contacts at the Pentagon and waited my time until I could be certain that the Walter Reed lawyer couldn't sanction me. I was within one month of my honorable discharge date, and I was counting every day.

Within a few weeks I was traveling twice a month up to New Haven to study for my MBA. I was able to do so thanks to the new GI Bill that Lieutenant Rieckhoff had spearheaded with his organization, the IAVA. It was an incredible opportunity, and invariably I wound up sitting next to all these interesting people on the train on my way up the East Coast. One day I happened to sit next to the director of the Iraq oil field development for the World Bank. He was a very collegial and kind man, but I was scared shitless sitting that close to him. Somehow the paranoia of combat hadn't worn off fully, and I just kept picturing the railway car exploding mid-trip. You couldn't pay me enough to wear that man's shoes. He had already survived multiple assassination attempts both inside and outside of Iraq.

I exchanged some pleasantries with him as best as I could in Arabic, and then I moved as far away from him as possible. I made sure I found another seat that, tactically speaking, was upstream from his railcar. No need to be paranoid enough to move to a different car before a blast only to realize too late you're downstream from the derailment.

On another trip, I sat next to a thirty-year veteran of the CIA who worked on the board of directors for one of the large defense contractors we had challenged. He was very encouraging about the fundraising challenge, and he thought his company ought to step forward to match the funds we had raised. He personally circulated the challenge among his colleagues on the board of directors and forwarded materials for our foundation to his community relations department. We also heard back from three of the other leading DoD contractors, so we knew the big contractors were definitely getting our message. Although we didn't receive funding, we could tell our persistence was finally reaching senior levels.

In fact, the replies we started to get from the contractors were...well, they were cute in their own little way.

Representatives from General Dynamics wrote back to tell us they weren't sure if they could match our fundraising efforts because they were concerned we would overrun their budget. Apparently a company with twenty-seven *billion* dollars in revenues was afraid of the awesome fundraising power that two grunts held. I just loved that answer. It made me feel like Superman. I kept the e-mail for my grandchildren to see someday.

Representatives from a French oil company, Total, wrote back to tell us they liked our proposal but unfortunately their laws precluded them from contributing to our foundation. The director of Lockheed Martin's community relations department ended up playing in a community volleyball league I played in, and I asked her group several times if they could contribute to the project. Her group also apparently couldn't match our awe-inspiring budget and fundraising prowess.

It seemed like everybody was smiling, wishing us luck with the endeavor, but not writing checks. It didn't help that the bottom had fallen out of the economy, and Bernie Madoff destroyed the endowment funds for numerous charitable organizations. I did happen to notice, though, that each of the firms we challenged managed to make their lobbying payments that year. They also managed to fund multiple think tank organizations in town that found ways to publish "white papers" from "academic experts" who argued for the escalation of our wars.

Around Christmastime, I was attending the annual business school ball at Yale when John Knight and I had a chance to catch up a bit again. We talked on the phone and joked about old times as we were both continuing to adjust to life back in America. He had a year and a half to go before retirement and was settling back into the routine with his family and his wife, Sara. I told him I was actually dressed in a tuxedo while we were talking, hanging out in a social setting that was just like life with the "five-o-Deuce" in the dungeon.

I sent him a picture from the evening's event with the group of professors and deans in their tuxedos. The banquet also had a string orchestra, crystal chandelier, and gourmet buffet to mark the occasion. It was all capped off by a champagne toast, and as we toasted I couldn't help but feel out of place in the incredibly privileged environment. I couldn't get past the guilt I felt that my brothers in other units were still downrange at that very moment. Later that night, John got the pictures I sent him from the banquet event. He wrote back jokingly, "Yeah, man, it looks just like the Deuce—minus the rockets, snipers, horseflies, and rivers of shit." As usual, John knew exactly what I had been thinking.

During the Christmas ball, I spoke with a few physicians from the medical school and they got me in touch with another surgeon at Yale. The surgeon at Yale, as was the case with countless other physicians, eagerly agreed to help operate on any child we could evacuate. I had been working for some time to try to bring a child out of Afghanistan, but it seemed to be even more difficult than Iraq. I had written back to the senior surgeon that the general at the Pentagon had recommended, but it seemed that even someone at his level didn't have the cross-agency influence to coordinate the evacuation. In all reality, though, evacuating kids for surgery was likely just way too insignificant an issue for his level of authority. Once again it didn't really fit into his lane, and fell between stovepipes of different agencies in our government.

In many ways it felt like we were always pushing the boulder uphill just to connect the obvious resources we had to work with. We still had a huge database of volunteer surgeons and the database of kids who needed help. We just kept plugging away, trying to make the connection between the two.

* * *

One day I got an e-mail from our dean at Yale informing us about the next guest lecturer we would have speaking to us at the business school. The list of speakers so far had been absolutely incredible. The dean had brought in leaders from cabinet-level federal agencies to speak to the business students over lunch. We would sit and eat lunch in a casual setting alongside a handful of students, and yet we would have the chance to learn from individuals who wielded authority over massive organizations—from the National Institutes of Health to NATO and the State Department. It was astounding to think how much they could change with the work they did every day.

One day the dean told us that CEO of a Fortune 500 company was going to come and speak to the group of us. At first I wasn't sure why the CEO's name sounded familiar to me. I read the message a few times before it dawned on me that the CEO was one of the defense industry leaders that John and I had written to from Baghdad asking for help with our fundraising challenge. His company handled a critical but relatively obscure business during the war, and as a result his company had come up on the list of leading DoD contractors we challenged.

I have to admit I was not happy when I first realized the CEO would be speaking to us. There is a saying in business that behind every great fortune, there is a crime, and I felt like that was the case with this CEO. I had come to Yale specifically because its business school faculty was adamantly dedicated to training business leaders who acted in a socially responsible manner for society. Yale had spent years pursuing ethics as the cornerstone to business and leadership. It distinguished itself by carefully avoiding the shortcuts that some of its counterparts had taken with sloppy practices and "Enron"-type teaching. The Yale business school was known for creating business leaders who were deeply committed to ethics in everything they pursued. Yet, there we were, preparing to listen to a lecture from a business leader who was arguably the single largest profiteer from the wars in Iraq and Afghanistan. I was not pleased.

I sent a message out to my classmates about the CEO's profits from the war, and they all knew that I was planning to confront him *mano-a-mano* during his lecture. One of my classmates even helped me set up a video to show what would transpire, as I was not going to back down from the opportunity to ask him why he had ignored the fundraising challenge letter we sent him from Baghdad. In my mind, I was preparing for battle again. I was preparing—finally—to confront a leader in person about the profits he had gleaned from war. As the lunch-hour lecture approached, I felt the same kind of adrenaline coursing in my veins as I had back in Baghdad. Although I wasn't wearing my body armor this time, my heart was pounding in my chest in exactly the same way. If only I had my weapon, I would have felt more comfortable.

As I walked into the lunchtime lecture, the first thing I noticed about the CEO was that he reminded me of the kind, elderly patients I treat in the hospital. I was caught completely off-guard by how gentle and soft-spoken he was. He shook my hand and said, "You must be Dr. Heavey. I read your bio, Doc, and I have to say thank you." At first I thought he was offering the kind pleasantries that most civilians afford to veterans, but he went on to tell me a personally profound and confidential story that, quite frankly, left me completely stunned. Like my dad, he was a Navy Vietnam veteran. He had seen the shit. He had been outside the wire, and he had family members who had also been outside the wire. In fact, his son was deployed as we were speaking even after earning a purple heart in a prior combat tour.

He went on to tell me very personal stories from his family that left me completely speechless. In no more than two minutes, I went from preparing for battle to realizing the man before me had already known the very path I was walking in. He spoke candidly about what his life had meant to him and the experiences that he held most sacred. I sat through the rest of the lunch too stunned to believe what had just transpired. I felt like Darth Vader had just told me he was my father.

The CEO had apparently never received our letter from Baghdad. Given the size of his organization, I thought this was definitely a possibility, as much as I had hoped someone would recognize the gravity of our message and forward it to his officers. He made a personal donation to the foundation a few weeks after our conversation and, in so doing, became the first business leader to step forward and make a tangible commitment. He was the first CEO who understood what we were doing, and he made a personal contribution to help our cause. He was a Yale alumnus as well, and I was grateful to see that a meaningful commitment to ethical business practices was still very much a part of the alumni community.

CHAPTER 18
THE EXPERIMENT MUST CONTINUE

As my coursework continued, I started to develop a more advanced understanding of how business and political leaders shape our society. I had always been fascinated by the overlap between the two, and as the school year went on, I began to appreciate a much broader understanding of how they interact. One of our classes was taught by Doug Rae, a professor who co-teaches a course called "Faith & Globalization" with former British Prime Minister Tony Blair. Professor Rae is a wonderfully engaging gentleman who welcomes the students in his class into his home. He gives most of his lectures in his kitchen and living room. It was rumored on campus that he had taught some of Yale's most prominent alumni, including Senator Kerry and our prior illustrious president. I was amazed to have the opportunity to listen to his lectures. It was always fun to imagine being seated alongside the students who had taken his class over the years.

Professor Rae talked about the history of the balance of power in Europe, and the European wars that eventually led to the development of the nation-state. He defined the nation-state, as an actor, by the boundaries in which the central government "holds a monopoly on the authority for the legitimate use of power to execute violence." I found this to be a particularly compelling definition, as it strikes at a matter that seems to be completely taken for granted in America. We just assume that our centralized "Leviathan" military always has the power to dwarf any local militia that might try to promulgate violence inside our own borders. In Iraq, there was no Leviathan, and nobody held the monopoly on the legitimate use of violence. If anything, we franchised the old monopoly it into a thousand different localized subsidiaries. Dirty militias were everywhere—everyone clung to anything they could for survival.

We spent time in Professor Rae's class exploring the nuances of property rights, the Coase theorem, and other economic principles that impact our national development. The overarching theme was that humans must be structured in societies where we can achieve cooperative gains from interacting with our fellow humans, rather than risking further danger to ourselves. In the middle of Iraq, that often seemed like a fantasy to me. To think that any two individuals could coexist and achieve "paretto optimum" on their "utility curves" by cooperating with one another seemed like an alien concept. To speak of it in a professor's home in an academic discussion half a world away was quite a change, but one that gave me even greater understanding of the lessons at hand.

I once treated a man who killed his cousin in order to steal his tank of kerosene. He had been hungry and cold at the time, so he had to murder someone in his own family in order to eat and stay warm. Having seen something like that gave me a powerful appreciation of why societal structures must be carefully crafted and maintained. If cousins would kill their own cousins to survive, it is obvious that humans are cunning animals when we are pushed to our limits. We just rarely ever see what those limits truly are.

Professor Rae's was the first in a series of eye-opening classes. Shortly after his class, we took another course on institutional power dynamics taught by Professor Cade Massey. The lessons Professor Massey taught were pertinent to a number of situations I had experienced with the chain of command in the military. In fact, his teaching was a major inspiration for me to write this book.

Professor Massey explored a political science study by Graham Allison that investigated models of power inside Washington. Allison's thesis breaks the models of power into three major types, one of which explores turf wars for resources at the cabinet level. I found this model to be particularly compelling after I had the opportunity to meet with officials at USAID and a nonpartisan organization known as the USGLC (US Global Leadership Coalition). USGLC has been a staunch supporter of "smart power," or the use of American resources to build international relationships by using policy tools like development and diplomacy alongside defense. It works with USAID, which is closely affiliated with the State Department on a cabinet level.

Our State Department is designed to harness the positive elements of human nature to enable nation building throughout the world. Since 9/11, our State Department has been dwarfed by the influence of the DoD and military operations from a budgetary perspective at the cabinet level. The State Department budget in the last decade has been less than one-tenth the budget of the DoD. In fiscal year 2010 alone, state and

USAID received $52.8 billion, while the DoD received $685 billion—without even counting war supplements. Secretary Gates at the Pentagon once famously observed that there are more members of military bands than there are diplomats in the State Department. This creates a situation where the public face of nation building has become our DoD operations, even though our DoD assets are trained for state-to-state warfare and destruction.

Infantrymen are not diplomats any more than diplomats are infantrymen. A diplomat would be killed in a heartbeat if he wandered outside the wire without the tactical knowledge of an infantryman. Similarly, infantrymen know little to nothing about international trade arrangements or cultural anthropology considerations in nation building.

According to Graham Allison's models of power in Washington, the imbalance between our State Department resources and our DoD resources on a budgetary level speaks volumes about our national priorities and the relationships in the cabinet. State has been pushed to the rear for far too long, and as a result a generation of foreigners now equates "American" with infantrymen wandering their streets with M-16s. I love my eleven bravo brothers more than anything, but I do not expect them to go play patty cake and make friends in hostile theaters of war.

These kinds of insights from the Allison studies were fascinating for me to see, although one day in Professor Massey's class we stumbled upon an even more interesting study pertaining to institutional power and authority. The study revolved around what is known as the Milgram experiment.

The Milgram experiment was designed to show that we, as humans, are hardwired to accept and defer to authority figures in our lives. The concept makes sense from a basic survival standpoint. As tribal cavemen we had to defer to the leader of the pack to be certain the tribe could survive in the wilderness. That instinct carries through to our existences today, where every day we defer to authorities in our lives. While it is easy to think this instinct doesn't apply to oneself, there is an overwhelming body of evidence to support it.

For example, we defer to traffic police to avoid car accidents, and we defer to physicians to make medical decisions for us. Dr. Milgram studied these simple instincts to show how institutions can use the basic wiring in the human brain to manipulate individuals to perform actions that would otherwise be morally reprehensible. His work was originally used to help explain how individuals could be manipulated to perform horrific behaviors like the mass murders in the Holocaust. Ultimately the evidence from his study has been cited across countless environments. Invariably the results are the same, and they highlight how a centralized institutional authority can wield great influence over the human psyche.

In his study, Dr. Milgram fooled a volunteer into thinking that he was participating in a study about education. He told a volunteer that he had been randomly assigned to be the "teacher" in an experiment alongside another volunteer who was the "learner." The learner, however, was actually a coconspirator in the study with Dr. Milgram. Dr. Milgram wore a laboratory coat and told the volunteer teacher to administer a series of electrical shocks to the learner. The learner sat behind a small wall out of direct view but within earshot.

The volunteer teacher—who was the real subject of the study—was told that the point of the study was to help the learner study more effectively. The volunteer teacher was told that the shocks would not harm the learner in any way. He was also told he had to shock the learner with progressively more powerful shocks any time the learner failed to give the right answer. Dr. Milgram went out of his way to explain to the volunteer teacher that the study was for education and the good of society.

As the study progressed, the volunteer teacher would continue to administer shocks until the learner started to pretend to shout out in pain. Invariably the teacher would turn to Dr. Milgram and ask if he should continue to shock the learner. Dr. Milgram would reassure the teacher in many ways. He would tell the teacher that the shocks might be transiently painful, but that they would do no damage. When the teacher objected again, he would tell the teacher that as the study supervisor, he held sole responsibility for the study and that the teacher had to continue to administer the shocks. Every time the teacher objected, Dr. Milgram had a reassuring and logical answer that would prompt the teacher to continue. Every time, he would conclude his discussion with the teacher in a calm and eerily sanguine voice, stating, *"The experiment must continue."*

Despite the fact the learner could be heard shouting in agony as the shocks increased in intensity, a stunning percentage of the teachers continued all the way through the experiment. The learner could ultimately be heard shouting, "Stop, stop, I have a heart condition!" yet the teachers continued to administer the shocks just as they were advised. It is mind-boggling to watch the video as the experiment unfolds. Occasionally the teachers themselves would shake their heads in disbelief, but then they would continue onward and shock the learner exactly as they were ordered to do by Dr. Milgram.

As an outside observer, it is easy to watch the video footage of the study and think that you would be one of the rare volunteers who refused to follow Dr. Milgram's instructions. But even without formal mechanisms to wield his power and authority, Dr. Milgram convinced an astounding percentage of the participants to continue to administer the shocks. It was such a profound demonstration of the power of institutionalized authority that related studies in the field have not been allowed for fear of harm to the subjects.

Dr. Milgram only scratched the surface of the power and authority that can be wielded in institutional settings. Everyone knows that senior leaders in the military have extensive legal and formal channels for authority that are a necessary part of the chain of command. I don't intend to dispute the necessity of such an arrangement—it is in fact the only way that our men and women can fight and survive in combat. Formal institutional authority is an absolute necessity, and I am extremely grateful for it. It kept me alive in Iraq.

But the challenge is that institutional authority holds the power to change your lens of perspective until you stop thinking independently. A perfect example of this came about recently when a video was released that showed combat footage from an Apache assault helicopter in Iraq. In the video the pilots shoot and kill men who were working for the Reuters news agency in Iraq. During the carnage, two children are also critically wounded.

When the video was first released to the public, there was a considerable amount of outrage, especially since the pilots can be heard congratulating each other as they kill the group of men. The outrage was quite understandable from a civilian perspective. As a civilian looking at that video, I would have been mortified to hear soldiers from my own military celebrating the fact they had just killed other human beings. To a casual observer who had never seen combat, their callous commentary is totally morally repugnant.

But when I watched the video after returning from Iraq, I had the same reaction the pilots did. I saw the pilots shooting grown men who were walking around a street battle wielding AK-47s and RPGs. The fact that the men who were killed were "reporters" for Reuters meant nothing to me—we came across corrupt interpreters and "reporters" all the time who were really just spies for JAM. I saw little difference with the Reuters correspondents, as they were clearly armed and wandering around during an urban street battle. They didn't have any giant "I'm a friendly guy, please don't kill me" tags on. Just the opposite—they were carrying weapons in a combat zone. They looked exactly like the roving gangs of thugs who tried to kill our men in the streets—peeking around corners and hiding behind obstacles, completely unaware that the eye in the sky was watching their every move.

Just like the pilots, I felt vindicated when they killed the Reuters reporters. I immediately identified with the fear I had felt when I used to watch herds of armed men wandering the streets outside my base. Our Apaches were our saviors— blasting cannons from half a mile away to kill the roving herds that were trying to kill us with RPGs and mortars. As much as I had been disconcerted in the chaos of our night-stalking missions, I remember all too clearly how grateful I was that the awesome powers from the air were on my side to protect me.

My lens had shifted to the point I didn't give a shit about the men who were killed. I fuckin' *celebrated* that they were killed. I even laughed when I noticed that the ground convoy drove right over the limp and lifeless bodies when they responded to the scene. I was certain that wasn't an accident. Some eleven bravo driving the Humvee knew full well his tires were going to mutilate the hearts and minds of the haji motherfuckers they had just killed, just like they did for pancake man. Unless you have known the pure hatred of combat, that kind of callousness sounds completely irrational and utterly inhumane.

All of this taken together made the video footage from Dr. Milgram's experiment especially compelling to me. The commander in Iraq who gave the orders to kill the Reuters journalists was, in effect, telling the pilots to "shock the learner," just like Dr. Milgram had instructed his volunteers. He had rational and legitimate reasons for his order, and the pilots executed his orders exactly as instructed. The institutional authority worked exactly as it was designed to work. The parallels to the Milgram experiment were identical. To an outside observer, the results are mortifying. To an inside participant, they are completely rational, even idealistic in nature.

There was one element of the Apache assault video, though, that went largely unnoticed in public that immediately jumped out at me. Shortly after all the carnage, the ground convoy approaches the scene of the aftermath, and they realize two children have been maimed in the fighting. The first ground medics responding on the scene can be seen running frantically with limp and critically wounded children in their arms. They can be heard over the radio, desperately radioing for medical evacuation to the local combat support hospitals. The medical evacuation is denied and no further explanation is offered.

When I saw that, it all came back to me again.

Even though, mercifully, I never had to resuscitate a child in an acute blast on our base, I had run into the same kind of resistance for other cases on plenty of occasions. Our medical rules of engagement always seemed to be built by design to restrict the access that local nationals—including children—had to our combat support hospitals. There are legitimate reasons the policy exists, but unfortunately the result is a default answer of no.

The video documented the reality that MEDROE can be used as an excuse not to treat local nationals, even in an acute setting like the one in the video, where their lives were clearly threatened. Although I never had a child brought to me immediately after being shot, the children I saw all had terrible medical problems. Invariably the answer from the CSH was that it was someone else's problem to figure out. The CSH directors have their hands full duct-taping together a hospital to resuscitate soldiers. They are not the Taj Mahal for locals who have no health care.

When I saw that piece of the assault video, I was again struck by the parallels to the Milgram experiment. John and I had fought like hell to bypass the MEDROE by building the foundation, and that caused a disruption in the institutional authority structure. We had tried to find ways around the policies and instructions we had been given. We were fighting not to mindlessly "shock the learner." It was no longer surprising to me that we had run into resistance at so many different levels along the way. We were questioning the institutional authority. We were questioning why "the experiment must continue."

After seeing the Apache assault video, I wrote an article for the National Security Fellowship that wound up being published through a couple of different news outlets. I felt compelled to write it because of what I had learned from the Milgram experiment in Professor Massey's course. I wanted the public to understand how the details of MEDROE are implemented in tactical situations:

Huffington Post Op-Ed: Kids Shouldn't Be Collateral Damage

Last week, frontline combat footage from an Apache helicopter was released to the public. After watching the clips, I sat wishing I had been surprised by what I saw. But I wasn't. Having rolled outside the wire in combat myself, I have to admit that the carnage did not strike me as anything beyond the brutal reality of war. What I was struck by instead is a detail that is largely left out of the video.

At the end of the clip two line medics can be seen desperately running with wounded children in their arms. Their commander, "Bushmaster Seven," is urgently requesting a medevac (medical evacuation) to the Rustimiyah combat support hospital. His requests are denied. Which raises the critical question— who was the officer at Rustimiyah who denied the transport? And why?

Few leaders realize that our medical rules of engagement—MEDROE—severely restrict the treatment of local nationals in our combat support hospitals. There are some legitimate reasons for this policy. For example, what do you do with a child whose parents are killed in battle? That's just one of many questions that are not so easy to answer.

Having served as a battalion surgeon, however, I can vouch for how infuriating it is to turn away a child in desperate need of help. It ran counter to everything I stood for as an American soldier, and it is in serious conflict with the Hippocratic oath.

Technically the MEDROE allow evacuation for cases where "life, limb, or eyesight" are threatened, but only during "acute resuscitation." Functionally, most forward medical assets are not equipped with pediatric trauma resuscitation supplies, so it makes little difference how hard you try to work around the MEDROE. Pediatric trauma resuscitation is arguably the single most complex medical scenario imaginable, with extremely difficult anatomy for invasive techniques like a thoracotomy (e.g., "cracking the chest"). In an American university hospital there are typically over fifteen experts involved in resuscitating a single child.

Yet when we have the highest imaginable responsibility to care for a child in combat, the lowest-level line medics are left to fend for themselves without support from higher levels of care. A line medic is typically a junior enlisted soldier who has to convince a senior medical officer to risk assets by sending medevac help into a "hot" landing zone. The default policy is to play it safe and minimize the assets at risk. Officers are not rewarded for taking a chance—even if it costs us the opportunity to live up to our values as Americans. Tragically it is children caught in the crossfire who pay the price.

As a way to solve the problems associated with MEDROE, my fellow infantrymen and I set up the legal infrastructure necessary to bypass the restrictions in our sector in Iraq. Since the Red Cross and major NGOs had fled the violence, we set up a nonprofit foundation to function inside the combat zone. In the process we overcame countless hurdles to evacuate stabilized children for life-altering surgeries.

The hurdles, sadly, were not just the considerable tactical obstacles involved in combat. In fact, the most troublesome challenges came from our own federal regulatory officials. When we were told that we were not allowed to submit nonprofit grants, we challenged the largest DoD contractors to match the funds we had raised. To date no company has matched the funds that a handful of infantrymen raised among their friends and families.

Army Field Manual 3-24, the counterinsurgency manual, dictates that it is a leadership imperative to take the initiative to solve problems that soldiers witness in the field of battle. FM 3-24 also dictates that "logical lines of operation" among all actors—military and civilian, private and public—must be synchronized to deliver relief to local national populations. Despite incredibly difficult obstacles we embraced the Army ethos— improvise, adapt, and overcome—to execute that mission. The Hope.MD Foundation has surgeons standing by from Dartmouth, Yale, Columbia, and numerous other universities offering to help mitigate the horrors of war.

Perhaps someday the DoD contractors will accept our challenge and help alleviate these disasters. Or perhaps someday a serious discussion of our MEDROE will help give hospital directors the resources they need to truly open their doors for care. Until then, we will continue to believe in American ideals, and the hope they can bring to mankind.

This may sound strange, but I realized soon after I wrote the piece that I felt like an idiot—like a narcissistic Boy Scout—for writing publicly about the issue. Despite our commitment to find a solution to the problems we saw, I felt like I was violating the rules of the military fraternity by speaking out publicly about the issue. It was ironic, since the guys I served with all encouraged me to step up and write the article.

It turns out the only person who had planted that instinct in me not to speak out, in a way, was Dr. Milgram. I had been taught in officer basic training that public comments were not authorized. That had been reinforced by the lawyers who warned me about "red flags" after the *Washington Post* reporter ran the article about our foundation. I had been taught in countless ways by the institutional authorities that members of the fraternity always stick together and survive by staying in the pack. Members of the fraternity don't publicly question the bullshit they see. Members of the fraternity ought to be afraid that they will be outside the fraternity the moment they open their mouths.

If there is one thing I value more than anything else in this life, it is staying in the fraternity alongside my brothers in arms.

It has taken me this long to finally figure out that I will be in that fraternity no matter what the institutional authorities may have ingrained in me. In fact, it is only because *they aren't in the fucking fraternity* that they go to such great lengths to convince those of us who are that we risk our membership if we speak up. It is the JAG lawyers, the generals, the admirals, the SES, the defense industry executives, the congressmen who are actually outside the fraternity. They are the ones who have never had the blood of their brothers on their hands, or a neglected child in their arms. I have. My brothers have. *WE* are the fucking fraternity. We are the members of the guardian class who have actually upheld our convictions.

I took a sacred oath of office when I joined the military fraternity, and as I walk around the Walter Reed campus now and see grotesquely disfigured young people, I no longer feel like an outsider. I've learned what it means to walk alongside my brothers and sisters in the combat fraternity, and I understand why Plato refers to it as the "guardian class" for society.

I have come to fully appreciate Plato's theory on the temptation of gold and the conflict it creates within the authority structures of the guardian class. The guardian class, in modern terms, has an exact parallel to the Milgram experiment. If your income and power are increased by fighting a war, there is little wonder why you would insist that the war must continue. When our leaders fail to remove themselves from self-serving conflicts of interest, they are advancing their own standing at the expense of my brothers in arms.

Our country's oath of office makes no mention of self-serving remuneration, or the temptation of personal advancement compromising a leader's integrity. A simple modification to the oath of office would transform how our guardian class functions, and in so doing, it would transform how our military and congressional authorities execute the work of our nation:

> *I, {state your name}, do solemnly swear that I will support and defend the Constitution of the United States against all enemies, foreign and domestic; that I will bear true faith and allegiance to the same; that I take this obligation freely, without any mental reservation or purpose of evasion;* ***that I will never advance my own interests above those of my countrymen, through financial or other means;*** *and that I will well and faithfully discharge the duties of the office on which I am about to enter. So help me God.*

When I took my oath of office, I was young and idealistic enough to think that something that simple would go without saying. I know senior leaders who would not hesitate to adopt that change in their oath of office, and I will follow them on missions through hell and back. The others can put up or shut up. Leaders lead from the front. It is rule number one in the locker room. It is rule number one in the fraternity. It is rule number one on the battlefield.

It ought to be rule number one in America.

EPILOGUE AND ACKNOWLEDGEMENTS

As this book goes to print the Yale University Hospital has allocated resources for reconstructive burn surgery on any child that can be evacuated from Afghanistan. This is the result of one and a half years of effort to replicate what we were able to build in Iraq. Thanks to an outpouring of support from donors and volunteers across the world, the Hope.MD Foundation continues to grow in size and scope. The Foundation continues to manage an expanding database of university surgeons who have volunteered to provide surgeries for children who are caught on the front lines of war.

I would not be here, and none of this would be possible, if it weren't for the love of my family and friends who have tolerated my irrational decisions for many years now. My wife, Melissa, has not only put up with raising two children practically on her own, she has tolerated countless household moves over the past several years. She is a saint who has put up with more hassle than any human should, and she has somehow managed to spread her contagious smile and boundless energy to every community where we have lived. I love you beyond words, Melissa.

John Knight, at this moment, is somewhere over the mountains of Afghanistan in a medical evacuation helicopter. Godspeed, brother. Another couple months and nobody can touch you. Thank you for everything you taught me, and for everything you did to help me survive on the other side of the world.

To my family: Mom, Dad, Beth, Monica, Karen, Brendan, thank you. You managed to keep Mom sane (by and large) while I was gone and convinced her to refrain from verbally accosting any public officials (that I know of). Thank you, Mom and Dad, for raising me to believe that anything is possible, and for showing me that it is.

Thank you to Mom (Sue) and Dad (Dave) Doan for everything you have done for Melissa and me and our little angels. I remember the picture I got in Iraq of the stitches for our eldest, and there is a special place in heaven for Nanny and Grampy who saved the day when she was hurt. Thank you for always being there for all of us.

Thanks to my brothers in the Deuce and elsewhere who are still out their fighting: Carr, Panduro, Shanklin, Beaubien, Parker, Chasteen, Mullen, Allred, Wakeman, Garcia, Hess, Logan, Benson, Snapp, Bodiford, Broward, Bhavsar (Sir), Stackle (Sir), Edgerton (Sir), Suchy, Avery, Churchill, Wolfe, Aswell, Zuniga, Giannaris, Milke, Ussery, Skiddis (First Sarn't), Walz, Cook, Gibson, Rosenfield, Gatson, Luckett, Kagger, Johnson, Sandmel, Eads, Dearborn, and yes, even you, Mansfield, you crazy SOB. I love you guys. May you rest in peace Albert B, Micheal M, Bryan B, and all our brothers we lost.

Thank you to my brothers at WRAMC who have kept me sane through it all, especially Mike Harrison, Big John Schlesser, and Anc Clarkson. Thank you Carney, Woslager, Zoller, Leatherwood, Jagger, Hendzel, Osario, Wilson,

Endicott, Gonzalez, Stubbs, Bob Kurlantzick, Rangu Murthy, Devon Davis, Richard, Hodges, Rita, Lyn, Leslie and Clint Black.

Thank you to Leslie Grabowski, Ted Achilles, President James Wright and Susan Wright, the Dartmouth and Yale communities, Dr. Akpek, Dr. Stotland, Dr. Butterly, Dr. Lazareff, Dr. Van de Wiele, and especially Nahid Tabatabai and Amin Plaisted. Thank you to the host families for all our other children that I never had a chance to meet or thank in person. Thank you to Rachel Gilliar for fifteen years of friendship and nonstop support. Thank you for an incredible amount of free legal advice and the professional risk you took to help an old friend.

Thank you to Ernesto Londono for risking your life to bring your incredibly important work to the world. Thank you to the senior generals who took the time to mentor and teach me about this world. Thank you to Tim Embree and Paul Rieckhoff at IAVA. Thank you to Brandon Friedman for many things, especially for convincing me to do this and standing with me in the fraternity.

For my little princesses, I love you to the moon and back. Thank you for understanding why Daddy was gone so much. Thank you for bringing meaning to my life. I love you, Goomba & Pooky.

APPENDIX: MILITARY ACRONYMS

11B's—eleven bravos, combat infantrymen

AO—area of operations

AWOL—absent without leave

BIAP—Baghdad international airport

BRAC—base realignment and closure committee

CAB—combat action badge

CERP—commanders emergency response program

CIB—combat infantry badge

CID—criminal investigation division

CIF—central issuing facility

CME—cooperative medical engagement

CODEL—congressional delegation

CSH—combat support hospital

DASD—deputy assistant secretary of defense

DFAC—dining hall

EFP—explosively formed penetrator

FLA—field ambulance

FNG—fucking new guy

FOB—forward operating base

FORSCOM—force command

HOC—humanitarian operations center
HUMINT—human intelligence
HVT—high-value target
IA—Iraqi Army
IAVA—Iraq & Afghanistan Veterans Association
ICMI—Iraqi Children's Medical Initiative
IDP—internally displaced person
IED— land mine
IPB—intelligence preparation of the battlefield
IRAM—mobile rocket/explosive device
ISF—Iraqi Security Forces
JAG—judge advocate general (lawyer)
JAM—militant Jaiyesh-Al-Mahdi Army
JRTC—joint readiness training center
JSS—joint security station
JTTR—joint theater trauma registry
KBR—Kellogg-Brown & Root
MEDCOM—medical command
MEDROE—medical rules of engagement
MOH—ministry of health
MOS—military occupational specialty
MRAP—armored vehicle
MRSA—methicillin resistant staph-aureus
MRE—meal ready to eat
NCO—non-commissioned officer
NGO—non-governmental organization
NIAC—National Iraqi Assistance Center
NVG—night vision goggles
QRF—quick response force
PAC—political action committee
PCI—pre-combat inspection

PROFIS—professional filler system
PRT—Provincial Reconstruction Team
PTDS—persistent threat detection system
REMF—rear-echelon-mother-fucker
RPG—rocket propelled grenade
S-2—battalion intelligence office
SAIC—Science Applications International Corporation
SEC—security and exchange commission
SES—senior executive service
SF—Special Forces
TOC—tactical operations center
TTP—tactics, techniques, and procedures
UCMJ—uniform code of military justice
USAID—US Agency for International Development
USGLC—US Global Leadership Coalition
VBIED—vehicle borne IED (bomb)

Made in the USA
Lexington, KY
01 October 2012